Behind Her Brand: Entrepreneur Edition Vol. 6

Compiled by Kimberly Pitts

Co-authored by:

Konni Spitzer

Sherry Neff

Myaann Payne

Leslie Zann

Dr Jane Torrie, DC

Lisa Pulliam

Charmaine Marshall

Ruthie Staalsen

Angie Leigh Monroe

Nikky Phinyawatana

Pearl Knapp-Chiarenza

Erin Weber

Behind Her Brand: Entrepreneur Edition, Vol. 6

1. Business 2. Internet

ISBN-10: 1542534968
ISBN-13: 978-1542534963
BUSINESS & ECONOMICS: Entrepreneurship

Thank you...

To the many inspired, committed and focused entrepreneurs who have a vision, message, and a clear purpose this book is dedicated to you. The pages were written with you in mind to provide you new perspectives, new approaches and new ways of looking at how you can continue on your entrepreneurial journey.

Thank you to the authors in this book that shared from your heart, your experience and from where you are today. Without your words on these pages, many would not know the blessing it is to be an entrepreneur.

TABLE OF CONTENTS

Your brand is much more interesting when it has heart and life behind it.

Behind Her Brand is a journey of lessons, obstacles, thought processes, disappointments, and victories that you go through when building your business. Creating your brand is much easier when you consciously infuse the breadth and depth of everything you do in what you make, so your experiences nourish your business brand.

Because, guess what?
The story of your brand matters.

Your audience wants to know how you started your business. How you came to be where you are at this very moment. They want to know what you like to do when you're not pounding the pavement with your brilliant work. They want to know about your path --- they want to know the person behind the brand. Then there's a really good chance they are going to trust you with their money.

Each of these authors share their obstacles, victories, and offer invaluable information that can help you grow, challenge yourself and look at your situations in a new light. I encourage you to learn from their stories and the lessons they have learned along the way to becoming successful entrepreneurs.

To Your Impact and Success,

Kimberly Pitts

Founder, UImpact & UImpact Publishing Group

KONNI SPITZER

Accessory Stylist with Premier Designs, Inc

Tell us a little about yourself. We want to learn about the person behind the brand.

I grew up on the grounds of the Lake Whitney State Park in the small Texas town of Whitney. I graduated from Whitney High School in 1987, after having completed all twelve years in the same school district.

I was an extremely shy child during my elementary school years, especially when adults would try to talk to me. However, I loved having my close friends over to play. As I moved into the awkward years of junior high school, I became interested in a variety of sports, but the one I loved the most was volleyball. Unfortunately, my high school coach required players to serve the ball overhanded. This was a significant challenge for me because I was so small. I was determined that I was going to do what she required so I could be on the team. It took many hours of practice during school and each day after school. My determination paid off and I accomplished that goal and started playing on the Varsity team as a freshman! I didn't realize it at the time, but my four years of high school sports taught me about hard work, determination, and teamwork. This was all preparation for the career I would choose later in life.

After graduating high school, I chose to work for a few years prior to obtaining my degree in Respiratory Therapy from McLennan Community College, in Waco, Texas. After obtaining my degree, I worked at St. Joseph's Hospital in College Station, Texas for several years before starting my career with Premier

Designs. This year I will be celebrating my 25th year with my company!

I am married to Chad Spitzer and we have a blended family of four sons: Kyle and wife, Courtney, Nathan and wife, Ashley, Wade, and Coleman. We are anxiously awaiting the arrival of our first grandchild, Lakyn in March of 2017.

Share with us what your business is and why you wanted to start this business.

I am an Accessory Stylist for Premier Designs; a high fashion jewelry company. I offer style sessions where I help ladies discover and develop their own personal style. These days there are basically two kinds of shopping experiences—in-store and online. With Premier Designs, I bridge that gap and bring the shopping experience directly to the consumer! Women are busy and wearing many hats, but I help them maintain an updated look and build their confidence through the "30 second" looks I teach them. All of this is done in the comfort of their home; office; local coffee shop or at lunch with their friends joining in on the fun.

One of the reasons Premier Designs was started was to allow moms to be at home with their children, while contributing to the family income through flexible work hours. My desire was to have a family, but I did not want to continue the 12-hour night shifts I was working at the hospital. Through Premier Designs, I was blessed to be able to work from home while my boys were growing up, which allowed me the opportunity to be very involved in all their sports and school activities, while at the same time building a successful home-based business.

What have you learned about yourself in running your business?

I have learned a great deal about myself by running my business. I have learned that I have qualities such as self-motivation, a strong work ethic, and the ability to work consistently and with integrity. I feel these are vital in growing a successful business. I am willing to seek wisdom and knowledge from those who are successful and who will encourage and mentor me. I have learned that you must have a plan or a system, and you must work that plan.

What 3 characteristics describe what has made you successful and why?

I feel the three characteristics that have made me successful are persistence, consistency, and my desire to be constantly learning. Being persistent helped me become successful because I continued my work and service despite difficulties and opposition along the way. I have developed consistency and determination because of Premier Design's constant example of integrity and strong work ethic. Their unchanging commitment to the core values upon which the company was founded has shaped the consistency and determination that have made me successful in my business. I have allowed myself to be teachable and willing to accept and implement the advice given to me by my mentors, as well as business and life coaches. When I started my career in 1992 in Premier Designs, I did not own a computer or cell phone, so I have had to learn how to use those tools as well as social media to enhance my business.

How have you defined your voice in your market?

When we look to try something different, we look to the experts. By specializing in fun and educational shopping experiences for over 25 years, I have learned what does and doesn't work. The best part is I've learned how to do this while making it a fun and interactive experience. Long gone are the days of sitting in your friend's living room watching a presentation. Now I come to your home, bring beautiful jewelry collections that fit your personal style, and personally help customize the "right look" for your style.

What would you advise someone who is struggling with building their brand?

My advice to someone struggling with building their brand would be to partner with a life coach or mentor to develop confidence and relational skills to interact effectively with others. Having confidence and belief in your products and the services you offer will develop trust in relationships and produce product loyalty as you network with others. Also, use these relationships to see what has or hasn't worked for those in your field in the past. Build off their successes and failures. You are not alone!

The other piece of advice would be to take risks. You might have to start small, especially if it is out of your comfort zone, as it was for me. With any risk comes the potential for great reward—so do something you haven't ever done before!

Staying motivated when things don't seem to be coming together is a challenge at times. How do you motivate yourself? What would you advise someone else?

To stay motivated, every 90 days I reflect on and evaluate why I started my business. My purpose is to enrich others' lives, so I look forward to building confidence in ladies through fashion and accessorizing. I also take time to look at our future goals—our dream home, vacations we want to go on, and spending time with our grandchildren. I am also motivated by being my own boss and having the flexibility to work my business around my family and other activities.

There have been days when it was hard—when I was ready to quit—but then I would get a call from a lady who needed encouragement and I was reminded of why I am doing this. Also, I can attend my son's music performances, or I can take a break to sit and have coffee with my parents, and I remember how blessed I am to do these things because of Premier Designs.

What has been your most effective marketing tool / strategy and why?

My number one marketing tool has been word of mouth. I have worked to present my product in a way that supports the company's values, but also creates a fun night out for ladies. When people have a good time, they tell their friends. When they have a new accessory in their wardrobe, they tell their friends. When they get jewelry collections for free, they tell their friends! By having a quality product with a quality reputation, the word will spread.

The strategy behind my brand is staying current with the latest fashions and styles. I do this in a variety of ways including researching magazines and television, and staying in communication with the people in my networking circle. One very effective marketing tool has been teaming up with a local fashion expert. Through our style sessions, we can collaborate and design the perfect look for any outfit. When she has a need for a style session "extra" I'm the person she turns to and vice versa. We market for each other!

What advice would you give to a woman entrepreneur who is ready to take her business to the next level?

First, I think it is important to believe in yourself. God created each of us to be special with different talents. We must be willing to develop and use them. We must also take risks. We must be willing to develop new business and branch out into new areas, without the fear of failure holding us back. Taking risks can be a frightening thing, but my mentor taught me to "do it afraid"! This builds confidence and with confidence there will be growth.

What "must have" resources would you recommend someone use in their business?

The first resource can either make or break a company, but either way it will set you apart from the competition. It is something you were hopefully born and raised with: strong moral values, honesty and integrity. I was always taught it's not what you do when everyone is watching, it is what you do in silence that matters. It is standing behind your product, making the right decision, even if it costs you money or even a lost customer.

The second resource is your circle. The best place to start is with the people you know. Are they supportive? Will they encourage you when times get hard? Are they willing to lend a hand, make an introduction, and support you at your events? Throughout these 25 years as a business owner, I have had people in my life who have done all these things. I have been blessed by people who would do anything to help make me successful, and this makes life and business much more fun. Through my job, I have had the privilege of not just gaining hostesses and co-workers, but making life-long friends—families we go on vacation with that I can't wait to see at the next event, or friends I meet for dinner or coffee and can do life with. This is the key behind any successful person.

What makes you a woman that is making an impact?

Through my upbringing, my experiences as a single mom, and Premier Designs, I can continue making a difference in others' lives. Growing up, my parents stressed the importance of giving back to others. We would do this by spending time at the local nursing homes, reading to the elderly, singing Christmas carols to those who were unable to leave their homes during the holidays, and so much more. As I began raising my sons, I remembered the importance of these activities and wanted to pass the same legacy on to them. Unfortunately, there were struggles along the way as I raised two boys as a single mom. There were times where I had to work multiple jobs to pay our bills but we did it! We learned the importance of leaning on each other and surrounding ourselves with encouraging people. Through Premier Designs, I could quit my other jobs and focus on this career. Today I get to enrich other lives through fun, fashion, and finances. I have been able to grow my team, helping many women just like myself.

However, there are two main ways I make an impact. The first is the legacy I am leaving through my sons. Second to God, my family is my priority. I have raised my boys in a Christian home, taught them the value of hard work and dedication, and as they grow, I have seen them continue to develop these qualities on their own. Along with my sons, we have started giving to those in need. Each year at Christmas we send a few deserving single moms a "Blessing Bundle" to not just help them financially but to encourage them; to let them know we recognize the work they are doing and to remind them they aren't alone. I used to only dream of the day I would be able to do this, but that dream has become a reality thanks to Premier Designs.

Learn more about Konni Spitzer

Konni Spitzer is an Accessory Stylist with Premier Designs, Inc., a high-fashion jewelry company. She is a busy wife and mother. Her passions include building confidence in women through laughter, fun and accessorizing.

Premier Designs has offered many opportunities for Konni, including the ability to work from home as she raised her sons after leaving the medical field. She started with Premier 25 years ago, and has been given the opportunity to be mentored by the Founders and President of the company.

Konni lives in Texas with her husband, Chad. Through his experience of owning his own company, they have continued to build and strengthen their team.

Website: www.premierdesigns.com

SHERRY (CALEY) NEFF

BoD Lashes and Esthetics
Certified Esthetician
Jeunesse Global Partner

Tell us a little about yourself. We want to learn about the person behind the brand.

My mother tells me I was born a leader. She wasn't sure what I would do with it but she encouraged me to "never sit out and always dance." Raised in a small town with little means and resources I hit the work force with no college education. I started with a startup company that grew quickly and I was fortunate to grow with them in their marketing department. I became good friends with the owners' son and at the age of 25 we started a business together in the auto recovery industry.

I married, divorced, and had 2 wonderful boys in the middle of starting my first company. I was left alone to raise my toddler children with no support of any kind. This was the hardest thing I had to face up to this point. But the experience made me stronger and bolder.

I married my current husband Raymond in 2005 and gained 2 more boys. We moved our family to Corpus Christi Texas in 2006 to expand my auto recovery business and open a small finance company. Raymond loved my entrepreneurial spirit and was so supportive of the future we had planned. However, a series of events changed everything.

We have faced more trials and endured more tragedy in the past 10 years than most people do in a life time. Starting with my youngest son being diagnosed with autism and betrayal from my longtime friend and business partner that would end in me losing my business. We felt it would be best for me to be a stay at home mom for a while. That is when I discovered network marketing. We started our first business Christmas night 2008 and quickly worked our way to the first 100 in the nation to hit the top level of the company. We were living the network marketing dream.

The next 8 years we faced tragedy after tragedy, including being terminated from our first company, fighting a law suit against us and losing all our income. It would take Raymond 3 years to find a job. We quickly went through our savings, cashed in 401K and pensions to live. When it was all gone, we filed bankruptcy and moved into our RV. We went from hero to zero so quickly and the stress was unbearable. I suffered from depression, began having anxiety attacks and my blood pressure was through the roof. I lost my desire and passion and became a person I hardly recognized.

Fast forward to today. Thanks to Jeunesse Global, I am healthy, happy and living the network marketing dream again. Raymond found a job and I went back to school, became a Certified Esthetician and opened a successful spa in Corpus Christi Texas where I feature the Jeunesse products.

Share with us what your business is and why you wanted to start your business.

Nothing causes health problems and aging quicker than stress. I no longer recognized the face in the mirror. I was being asked if I was my mother's sister and my sisters mother. My immune system was shot and I was constantly sick and fatigued.

One day I was invited to lunch with a friend I had not seen in months. The minute she opened the door she had an amazing glow about her. I couldn't believe how youthful her skin looked. She told me she was selling LUMINESCE a product of Jeunesse Global. She gave me a 7 day sample and after 7 days I was so excited to know more.

I could not believe how quickly Jeunesse changed the way I felt and looked. I became obsessed with turning back the clock for myself and others. I was having a blast with Wine and Wrinkle Parties and giving facials. I found my new passion. I wanted to show women how they too can conquer the adversities of life and look and feel amazing doing it.

My passion led me to enroll in school and become a Certified Esthetician giving me a second stream of income and a perfect platform to continue my success in Jeunesse Global. I didn't pause for a moment, graduated, passed my test and opened a Spa a week later. Jeunesse Global offers products to heal the body and skin from the inside out.

What have you learned about yourself in running your business?

I have learned that I am equipped with everything I need to be successful through life's toughest lessons and failure does not define me. I can succeed, fail and succeed again. And I love helping others do the same.

What three things do you wish you would have known when you started?

You're not in business alone! BUT....your direct upline might not be the best mentor for you. The world is full of amazing leaders. We all have strengths, weaknesses and comfort zones. Many times, your immediate upline is the total opposite of you and that is OK. Without disrespect, their leadership might not be the best leadership for you. Search for the mentor that will bring out your best. Once I figured this out and found mentors that I could relate to my business began to thrive.

You're in business for yourself! BUT....you are also at the mercy of corporate. You can build it and then lose it with a push of the button. So, respect the company you choose. Follow the rules. Read the fine print. Stay loyal. And remember the grass is USUALLY not greener on the other side. The more you prove success in network marketing the more "offers" you will get to switch companies. Be very careful with your decisions. Success is a long-term commitment.

Follow the System! BUT....find the version of the system that works for you. All companies and leaders have a system they follow. And that system works! For many. But you must take that system and break it down into a system that fits your lifestyle, direct network, personality, comfort zone and knowledge. I found that if you try to do something that doesn't sound or feel natural coming from you then you will have a hard time getting a positive response. The downside to this is that you also have weaknesses that you must work on to protect you from failure.

What 3 characteristics describe what has made you successful and why?

Determination! Wrap your head around the fact that everyone is offered the same opportunity in this industry. If the top person can make it, why can't you? We can come up with all kinds of reasons; she knows more people, she has lived here longer, she is prettier, she can speak in front of people, she is out going, she has experience....Bla...Bla...Bla! I promise you there is something you have she doesn't have. All she did was find HER strengths and figured out how to make them work for HER. Find yours! I was determined to study all the leaders in our industry and find those gold nuggets from each that might work for me.

Humility! In this industry, it is so easy to keep wrapped up in the "Hollywood" of it. Within each network marketing company are "celebrities." You can end up on websites, billboards, commercials, magazines and stages all over the world. People want to take their picture with you and even ask for your autograph. You can literally watch people change before your eyes. I know because it happened to me. And when it does you begin to think you're not appreciated enough, deserve more and begin to care less about others. It took me bringing us down to the depth of the trenches to know the person I had become. I have learned the importance of Humility. Humility attracts people. And people are our business. Love one another and support everyone.

Respect! I disappointed a lot of people on my journey because of lack of respect. It is important to respect yourself but it is equally important to respect others. When your honest, loyal and tell the truth you will gain the respect of others, while showing them the utmost respect. Like any industry, bad habits and characteristics evolve to take short cuts. Be true to yourself and others and you will find more success than you ever imagined.

How have you defined your voice in the market?

In the beginning my voice was hard working mother of an Autistic Son, willing to help everyone around her. Then the voice became pillar of strength, going through so much tragedy and pushing through. But now my voice is more gentle, caring and understanding.

What would you advise someone that is struggling with building their brand?

Educate yourself! Brand building is not something people are just born with. It takes learned skills. Learn from the best, pay the price and continue to learn every day. Don't be afraid to change your brand and rebuild if necessary.

Staying motivated when things don't seem to be coming together is a challenge at times. How do you motivate yourself? What would you advise someone else?

Getting motivated is a huge struggle when you own any business. For me motivation comes from setting tough goals and finding ways to make them happen. I set daily, weekly and monthly goals and adjust accordingly as I fall short or push ahead. I have these goals on a dry erase board in front of me always. I also set hours that I "work" and fill my schedule accordingly. I go to all corporate events, get on all corporate calls and study my website and business at least 5 days a week. I listen to self-development and look for new nuggets to incorporate. When you stay involved, motivation comes naturally.

What has been your most effective marketing tool/strategy and why?

Personality Profiling! There is a lot of good programs on the market. I studied Global Bank Academy with Cheri Tree. This changed everything I did and increased my success tremendously. I learned to communicate with people. We all have personality profile traits, good and bad. Which means we all communicate differently. By recognizing these traits, I learned to bring the best out of everyone. I learned to give different presentations, training, follow up, advertising and speeches per personality traits. I found that instead of having a great experience with a ¼ of the people I spoke with, I can now relate to just about anyone.

One of the biggest struggles women entrepreneurs have is how to price themselves. What advice would you give about pricing your services and offerings?

Biggest advise I can give to women who are trying to price their services or offerings is to not think for people. When you judge how people will react to your price you can easily sell yourself short. I love the saying "fake it till you make it". I am very good at this. When you meet with someone they only see what they see and hear what they hear. Dress and carry yourself according to the person you plan to be. No one knew I lived in an RV. They assumed I was successful even during my darkest days because that is the way I carried myself.

What advice would you give to a woman entrepreneur who is ready to take her business to the next level?

Prepare! Preparation is everything to move your business to the next level. Prepare the family! Get the family together and explain that extra hours are going to be put into your business. Share with them how important this is to you and their help is appreciated. Ask for their support.

Prepare your goals! If you don't make goals, you won't even understand how to make it to the next level. Small goals are more comfortable. Instead of saying I need 10 people this week to join my business, say I need to talk to 3 new people a day about my business. Achieve the small goal and the large goal will happen.

Prepare your team! Both upline and downline. Upline needs to know you have solid goals set and what you need from them to make these goals happen. Downline should be a part of your plan. Don't go alone take them with you. Figure out who is ready to work and work with them to make small goals and your goals will be made to.

Prepare to be accountable! Find someone who will hold you accountable for reaching your goals. Make this person someone who knows what it takes and can help you make it. Hire a coach if you are able.

What "must have" resources would you recommend someone use in their business?

The best resources are available right under your nose. Your company supplies you with everything you need. Don't try to reinvent the wheel. This will just waste time. Find a mentor you connect with. Revamp their "system" to fit your strengths. Always have business cards and marketing materials. Wear company clothing. Learn the art of three way calls. Keep goals in site on a white board. Participate in company events, calls and training. Have a planner that is used just for your business. Make sure you are filling it in with daily tasks. Even if it is just an hour a day.

What makes you a woman that is making an impact?

I am a survivor. I have faced more in the past 10 years than most woman endure in a life time. I understand what it takes and I want to help other women do the same.

I thrive to make an impact each day. I love the saying "I want to be the type of woman that when my feet hit the floor the devil says oh crap she's up!" Take advantage of each day. Always wear a smile and look for someone you can help.

My spa offers discounts for cancer survivors, senior citizens and students. Feeling beautiful gives you energy to keep going.

Wild Card Question. Share whatever you would like the women reading your story to know about you, your business or journey.

I have mentioned through my story that I was faced with trials and tragedy the past 10 years. Now I want to get more detailed with a timeline so that you can see where I came from, what I went through and how quickly I bounced back.

June 2006 – I developed a large fibroid in my uterus that had to be shrunk and then hysterectomy.

Oct 2006 - My youngest son Jaxun is diagnosed with autism. Not knowing what we were facing we pulled him out of school and waited 6 months to get into a neurologist.

Oct 2007 – My business partner and longtime friend began an affair with my 21-year-old receptionist. Something I could not live with. We decided to sell my business back to him. Taking a low settlement to get past it as quickly as possible.

June 2008 – We sold our dream house and downsized.

Dec 2008 – We started our first network marketing company. Moved up the ranks quickly to the 3 level of 5 in just 6 months.

Sept 2008 – My 37-year-old Brother died suddenly in his home.

Dec 2008 – Jaxun becomes very ill. Took us 3 months to figure out he had Type 1 Diabetes.

Mar 2009 – Jaxun is hospitalized with DKA (diabetic ketone acidosis). We spent a week in the hospital. Then had to learn how to care for him.

July 2009 – Made it to the 4th level of 5 in the company.

Sep 2009 – My cousin Mark dies in a tragic car accident.

Sep 2009 – My husband's nephew dies at the age of 18 in his parents' home from a drug over dose. A complete shock to everyone.

Oct 2009 – My father dies.

May 2010 – My husband and I take my 2 boys to a Memorial Day party. We were told we would have a tent for our family. But we did not understand the tent would not have any pillows and blankets. We attempted to stay but it was too uncomfortable. So, we made the decision to drive 20 minutes down the road to my husband's sisters house. Being a non-refusal weekend the police were pulling everyone over. My husband was arrested for DWI and because we had the kids he faced felony charges. This mistake costed us over $50,000 to make it right.

Nov 2010 – I was Black Friday shopping in the middle of the night when my sister in law talks me into trying a coffee with pumpkin spice cream. I have never drunk coffee before but this was good! I became highly addicted. But I did not know I was deathly allergic to the coffee bean and didn't put 2 and 2 together as I become very ill. The doctors were testing me for everything under the sun and could not figure out what was shutting my body down. It was almost a year before a chiropractor suggested a food allergy test. By the time, we figured out coffee was the culprit my body suffered damage. I was so full of toxins I remained sick. My immune system was shot and my thyroid damaged. I suffered from extreme fatigue for over a year.

Jan 2011 – Raymond was given the choice to either retire from his corporate job of 18 years or move to Rio Rancho New Mexico. With no desire to move and our Network Marketing Company thriving we decided to take the early retirement. He was offered to stay 2 years but would have to retire Sept 2013.

2011-2013 – Over these 2 years our Network Marketing Company began to make changes which took a toll on our income. By the time Raymond retired our income was not enough. We decided we needed a second income.

Sept 2013 – We decided to look at a company that was considered a competitor. Lots of people from our original company had moved over and they were doing well building this new company while still getting paid for the work they did for the first company. We were convinced we could do the same. So we did what we thought was right and called our first company to let them know. We asked to be vested, which meant we would no longer represent the first company but would continue to get paid for the customers we brought to the company. We were not told other wise and so we began working our new business.

Oct 15th 2013 – Our check did not hit the bank with our first company so I logged on to see what the delay was. What I saw on the screen took me to my knees! "YOU HAVE BEEN TERMINATED"! We called but no one would talk to us. The phone began to ring and everyone who switched companies was also terminated. With nothing we could do we worked over time to get our income up in our new business.

Nov 18th 2013 – We received a letter in the mail that the company was suing us along with 2 other leaders who left.

Nov 20th 2013 – My 31-year-old Brother was killed in an explosion in the Texas Oil Fields. I left the next day to be with my mom as long as she needed me. No mother should lose a child but now she has lost 2 in such a short period. I spent 3 months with her.

A few days after Thanksgiving our upline in the new company flew in to see us. Sat on our couch, met our children and told us to keep building and he would pay for the attorney to fight our first company.

Jan 2014 – We promoted to a leadership position with our new company and our income was starting to grow to 6 figures.

March 2014 – Mom and I decide to take a road trip. She wanted to go see her Mother in Tennessee. So we hit the road. We got all the way to Tennessee and was 1 day away from arriving at her house when we got the call that she died in her sleep. Our trip turned into another funeral. This threw us both into a depressed state and I needed some time off from building our new business. This slowed down productivity.

April 2014 – We could no longer pay our Mortgage. So we rented it out. We decided to move to Dallas, a bigger market to work our current business. We moved into a tiny apartment and continued to work.

May 2014 – After only making 1 payment to our attorney we were informed that we were no longer producing fast enough and no more payments would be made to the attorney.

June 2014 – We told our attorney we had no money and would not be able to continue to fight to get our income back. He notified the company and they settled with us but the settlement came with some stiff requirements. We had to cancel our current business and sign a 1 year non-compete agreement. We were now facing zero income. Raymond began searching for a job and worked construction to help. With no college education and over 20 years out of corporate America I could not get anyone to look at my resume.

Dec 2014 – I began taking medication for high blood pressure, anxiety and depression.

Jan 2015 – We file Ch 7 Bankruptcy

Aug 2015 – I start my Jeunesse business.

Sept 2015 – I break my leg

Sept 2015 – We can no longer afford the apartment and move into an RV

Jan 2016 – I start school to become an Esthetician

Mar 2016 – Raymond gets a job!

April 2016 – We move back to Corpus.

May 2016 – I graduate.

June 2016 – I open BoD Lashes and Esthetics in Corpus Christi
Today my business is thriving. Raymond has a salary again. And I am climbing the Jeunesse ladder. 2017 is our time to soar!

Learn more about Sherry (Caley) Neff

A small-town girl turned entrepreneur. Wife and mother of 2 boys, step mom of three kids. Homeschool teacher to her son with autism and Type 1 Diabetes. Sherry Neff started her first traditional company at age 25 and her first network marketing company at 39. Survivor to years of trials and tragedies which has taken her from hero to zero. She currently owns BoD Lashes and Esthetics in Corpus Christi, TX where she enjoys helping women feel beautiful inside and out while featuring her Jeunesse products.

Website: www.sherryneff.jeunesseglobal.com

MYAANN PAYNE

MYN Image & MYN Style Box

Tell us a little about yourself. We want to learn about the person behind the brand.

To tell you a "little bit about myself" is to tell you my whole (long) story so you get where I'm coming from, but for the sake of BHB I'll give you the cliff notes:

I'm originally from Texas, but I've lived in Los Angeles, Mexico, Phoenix, and I made my way back to Texas after saying I'd never live here ever again. I do faintly remember holding up a finger as I drove on I-20 West toward California at the ripe old and rebellious age of 16. I don't think I was exactly pointing so much as gesturing if you catch my drift. One finger in the air, but it was so long ago I can't exactly remember. Tee hee.

I've not always been outspoken and bold. In fact, for most of my life I was very timid and unsure about myself with every step I took. Never in a million years would I have ever thought I'd be the CEO of not one, but two businesses.

I love fiercely, and I am eager to help other women in business get a leg up. I am a little loud, love to make people laugh, and I try to be the light in a dark room. Since my little sister passed away in May of 2016, my perspective on life and the way we treat each other and ourselves has changed. Her death brought new meaning, understanding, and passion for what I do. "Life is too boring to wear ugly clothes" one meme circulated. I say, "Life is too short to have a closet full of clutter and clothes that don't work for you, making you wonder what to wear and repeat outfits for months on end, thus creating stress. You don't need that. Stress will kill you." I'm long winded also.

Share with us what your business is and why you wanted to start this business.

My business is personal branding. I help women (and men) develop and perfect their personal brand with the clothing they wear and their esthetic choices. Simplifying your wardrobe down to the essentials, and really honing in on the best version of yourself to put forth to the world is key.

This business came to light because I feel that every year the media has more influence over how we should be. How we should dress, act, look... (the Kardashian craze has GOT to stop) it's ridiculous. You open a magazine and see these women with their perfect aka airbrushed bodies, great hair and makeup, and expensive clothes. The big companies are telling us we have to be this way. We have to live a life of status. No one is perfect (let's not forget that Kim K has psoriasis) but the media puts so much pressure especially on women that I felt I must step up and try to change that.

So, my whole mission is to try and reverse the thinking. You don't have to be a toothpick, you don't have to wear Gucci everyday...hell, you don't have to wear the trends. It's not about ANY of that! I want all my clients to step out every day in an outfit that fits their body and their lifestyle, regardless of what the magazines say. It's about feeling great about yourself and having a closet of timeless pieces that will last you 5 years, not about striving for unattainable body goals and living in excess. Someone's got to break the cycle of overbuying and feeling unsatisfied/unfulfilled with their clothing, and why can't it be me?! To reach a bigger audience, I started a subscription box service in the summer of 2015. I gather info about my client's lifestyle and their measurements and I shop for them monthly.

What have you learned about yourself in running your business?

I've learned a lot about myself in the throes of running these businesses. Time management is by far the biggest lesson I've learned. I forgot to mention earlier that I also have a baby that was born 1/21/2016 and between the two businesses, the baby, the household, the husband, and oh yeah – myself; time management has kept me from falling off the deep end. Time blocking and being mindful of how I'm spending my time has been paramount.

I've also learned that I am not an executer. For so long, I struggled with bringing on help because well, "I can do it myself." Ok, well there are only 24 hours in a day and I had to sleep at some point. So, recognizing and admitting that I'm a high level creative, not an executer, then taking steps to work with that aspect is also a big lesson learned. Prioritizing is something I learned that I didn't do so well. Even though I'm still an incessant list maker, I am much better at prioritizing my tasks and to do list.

What three things do you wish you would have known when you started?

There are three things I SO wish I would've known when I started.

First of those three majorly important points is the time it would take before I cleared a profit; a true profit. The first year I was profitable, year #3, I made $321. Now, to just say "3 years" in passing doesn't seem like a lot, but when you go from a combined income of 90-100K down to 65K for those three years, it's a big leap. I wish I would've known it would take 4 years before I was profitable so that I would've saved more, we wouldn't have taken trips, we would've buckled down on spending, and I would've been more patient with myself.

My first year in business my goal was to make $40,000 and I didn't have a plan or any other true goals. The disappointment factor was MAJOR after year 1. We lost about $4,500 and were officially in debt. The second year, we lost about $3,000 and were even further in debt. Year 3 we started selling stuff we didn't need and were in debt almost $20,000. I made $321 though! Year 4, my husband sold his truck and the last quarter of 2016 I doubled my style box subscribers AND my client base. I cleared almost $4000 for the year in profit. In December 2016, I brought in as much money as my husband does monthly. Had I had a crystal ball to tell me to hang on, I wouldn't have wanted to give up so many times!

The second thing I wish I would've known from the get go is to hire a business coach. I hired mine in the 3rd year in business and from reading the numbers I mentioned a minute ago, you can see what a difference it made. I needed her guidance and ideas from the get go to build a solid foundation. I'm very much a "let's put on the roof" type and I don't even have up drywall, and the foundation is still wet concrete. She would've kept insisting that I let the concrete dry before starting to put in the walls on my business.

She also has given me the best middles of the cinnamon roll. Oh – you don't catch my reference? Well, I love cinnamon rolls. I don't know how you eat one, but I eat mine from the beginning of the swirl to the middle. It keeps getting better, but the most cinnamon sugar and icing lies in the middle of cinnamon roll. I will share any other part of my cinnamon roll with you, but not the middle. No ma'am, no sir. The middle of the cinnamon roll is reserved for that last satisfying bite…and that's what I get from my mentor/coach. The middles of the cinnamon roll. Invaluable information, tips, tricks, introductions…I wish I would've knew about her from the start.

The last thing I wish I would've known from the jump is how to spot time wasters. For starters, I'm long winded; I love people, I love to help, but I wasted time on projects and people that didn't align with my brand, my vision, and for sure were not a great use of time. I chased every shiny opportunity and would sit and talk for hours with people about all kinds of things, and it didn't get me anywhere. Too many non-mutual meetings…to the point that I sat down with another business owner for what I thought was a girlfriend's lunch and she basically squeezed me for info, tips and tricks, ideas on how she can grow her business by implementing new programs, etc. Then I found out that she used all those middles of the cinnamon roll I gave her that day to make thousands. I asked her if she was looking to hire a consultant for her business, and of course she said no. Well why would she if she got all those middles for free?! Eliminate time wasters, Myaann. Cut and paste them on a document entitled "Do Not

Open" and keep moving with it. Now I only meet with people for the mutual benefit of us both, people that are of the same driven mindset.

What 3 characteristics describe what has made you successful and why?

My passion, my honesty and integrity, combined with my styling method are the three characteristics that have made me successful. I'm fiercely passionate about giving my clients exactly what they want and need. I'm passionate about my core beliefs: dressing right for your body type and lifestyle above staying on trend.

I'm also passionate about my clients feeling good about themselves. They should be able to put on an outfit they love every single day. My honesty is in the fitting room "if you don't love it, don't buy it" is a common phrase I use; along with "if you keep saying you're fat, I'm going to leave." The latter I don't use as much, but I will whip it out when it's needed. I also think that I have a high level of integrity; I'd rather overspend on a Style Box than send a box of crap. My financial advisor may say otherwise, but I would rather cut into my profit than send something cheap or something that's not what they need or want.

My method of cleaning out, organizing, and shopping is different from other stylists. I don't go in and throw everything out and then drag them to the mall. I'm very methodical with what we weed out, and I never just blindly go to the mall to shop. I make appointments with the stores and have everything ready to try on before we even get there!

How have you defined your voice in your market?

Defining my voice in the market was hard at first because I didn't know what my voice WAS for the first two years in business. I knew nothing of the "know, like, trust factor." My voice is defined because I go against what the media and mass market retailers say. The retailers want you to spend money on a weekly basis; I want you to spend money on a quarterly basis. There's more value in your closet than you think and you don't need a whole new wardrobe. You need to re-work what you've got, weed out what doesn't work, replace and refresh. Plus, I cater to everyone, from a size 00 to a size 24+.I offer different packages for people with almost every budget, and of course the Style Box option also! Defining my voice is what really catapulted my business. Once I defined it, all my marketing became centered on it, and my message became clear.

What would you advise someone who is struggling with building their brand?

Here's a bit of advice for someone who is struggling in finding and defining their brand: strip it down to the bare bones. Why did you start your business in the first place? What is the fuel to your fire? What are you MOST passionate about? Start there and then figure out what makes you unique. Is it your quirky glasses? Do you only really wear a blazer, t-shirt, and jeans? Own it! Own whatever makes you different appearance wise and own what you're most passionate about. Then run with it! Don't ever forget that YOU are your brand…define YOU, and you've defined your brand. Find what qualities and traits about you that are different from everyone else. You can also dig deeper and peek at what other businesses in your space are doing. What are they doing wrong? That's a perfect starting point for you to fix what they're doing wrong and perfect what they (and you) are doing right.

Staying motivated when things don't seem to be coming together is a challenge at times. How do you motivate yourself? What would you advise someone else?

Getting bummed out is easy for entrepreneurs when we hit rough seas. Maybe not so much a rough sea but a salt flat: it's dry, it's boring, and ain't much happening. Throw in impatience and perfectionism and you've got a bummer cocktail. Shake THAT and strain over ice. I know this area well. I used to get bummed often. Stagnant is not a space I'm comfortable in. One way to combat this is having a few irons in the fire. That way, when one cools down, you can grab another one that's hot and strike it some more.

Another thing that will get you out of a slump is going to have an office day in an unusual place. At a café on the patio, at the mall. At a museum, perhaps. Somewhere with free Wi-Fi and maybe a bite to eat or drink. Getting out of your usual space will work wonders for your creative mind. Another cobweb clearer is to purge and organize. I am the best collector of scrap paper and lists written on bits of cocktail napkins, post it notes, and backs of receipts. When an idea hits me, I need to write it down! So, every now and then I gather all those bits and type them up in a document and file it in my idea binder. I will always get a surge of motivation to keep going when I do that.

Reading client testimonials does it for me also. Remembering that some people think I'm amazing and are appreciative of what I've done for them really is a confidence and motivation booster! If you don't have a plethora of client reviews and testimonials, well, add that to your vision board. Don't have one?! Create it for Pete's sake! You've got to have a point of reference. Put your "why" on there. Put a pair of shoes you want, a trip you want to take…type up business and personal goals for yourself. Make sure they're attainable, and feel the surge of positive energy sweep over you. If all else fails, go for a stroll or watch an inspiring documentary!

What has been your most effective marketing tool / strategy and why?

As for most the effective marketing tool? By far has been word of mouth. To get good word of mouth reviews, you've got to provide something stellar: a stellar product with stellar service. Word of mouth was more powerful than the money I spent on Yelp Ads, Facebook ads, and all the strife I endured posting 3 times a day on Instagram. Don't be afraid to ask for referrals. While someone is raving about your service or product to you, tell them, "I'm so glad you're happy with my product/service. If you know someone else in need of (insert your greatness here) please pass them my info! I'll send you some business cards if you need." Come up with a cool referral program and promote it big time! I got a client of mine a bottle of prosecco and a bouquet of flowers and I took a picture of it on her front porch and posted it with the caption "When my client sends me a referral, I take care of her!" and tagged her in it. Needless to say, she was elated to come home to something special just for her. It's the personal touches that will carry your business far.

One of the biggest struggles women entrepreneurs have is how to price themselves. What advice would you share about pricing your services and offerings?

Pricing yourself should be simple, but people have big issues with this. First rule of pricing yourself: KNOW YOUR WORTH. Why start a business if you aren't going to be profitable? People need you. Don't forget that! Now, a wise man once broke it down to me like this:

To figure out your price per hour you first total up all your bills, things you must pay every month, including savings/investments. Then figure out how much extra you want/need: i.e., nails done, hair done, shopping budget, going out to happy hour and leisurely lunches.

Add all that up. Add in a buffer to that. So, that's what you should be bringing in every month.

- How many hours do you want to work per week? Times that by 4.
- Divide the number of hours you want to work a week into how much you need to make per month.

Example: My goal is to bring in at least $8000/month. I ideally want to work 20 hours a week. So, my hourly rate is $100/hour for my personal branding clients.

Remember those irons in the fire? If I'm not working 20 hours/week with my clients, I shift and do some more promoting of my e-book or a specific package to get me to my goal.

Once you set your price per hour, do not discount it for anyone. Anyone that is not willing to pay you your hourly rate is not your client. That goes for products too. Your product costs you X and you need to make Y to keep your lights on. If one person is trying to negotiate with you on your price then they don't see the value, and therefore are not your customer. The end. There are plenty of people in the world that will pay you what you're worth!

What advice would you give to a woman entrepreneur who is ready to take her business to the next level?

If you are ready to take your business to the next level, then hooray for YOU!!! It's so exciting to grow. The feeling of validation and accomplishment is amazing. A bit of advice for taking the next step up: find people that hang out in your next level space. I'm not talking about going to a stale muffin and cold coffee 6am networking meeting where you wear a sticker nametag. I'm talking about real schmoozing here. Go to cultural activities or events that coincide with your product or service. For example: I have a friend that is in a direct sales company and their thing is books. Most of the reps just have the parties in their home, invite their friends, and yawn…boring…blah. No. I told her to partner with her local kid friendly fast food chain owner and see if she could set up a table. Bring some of the books for kids and parents to see. Take some orders and sell some books. Do it enough times and people will go there to see what new books you have. Not only will she sell books to her target audience, she can build her business by networking with the moms that are there already. She's already engaged them, why not get to know them and see if it would be something they'd like to do in their spare time? Boom. She leveled up the first month. True story.

Go where your target market is. Go against the grain. Think outside the box and think global. Think mass market. You will get to your next level faster than you think, then you'll get to the next level even faster!

I would suggest you hire a business coach. Someone that specializes in marketing. Someone that will tell you the truth, even if you don't like it. Someone that you respect and trust and moreover, someone who has your best interest at heart! Being pushed and challenged is a good thing and is essential for growth and leveling up.

What "must have" resources would you recommend someone use in their business?

There are some must have resources that you need in your business. Here are my top five:

1. QuickBooks Self Employed – I should've put this in the section about things I wish I would've known to start with. This tool has been invaluable to me not only does it show my income and spending habits (I sorely needed to see those charts that are red to indicate over spending) but the app on your phone tracks mileage. You can take pictures of all your receipts and it makes filing your business taxes SO much easier! I can't say enough good things about this program.

2. Square – it's a portable cash register. All you do is download the app, connect your bank account, and get you a card reader. Or two or three. I have several that are stashed away just in case I don't take my handbag. It also helps to have a Square Space website so all your payments kind of go to the same place

3. SMS Scheduler – yes. Schedule your text messages. I text my clients to confirm appointments, but I can't always remember to do it. Come to think of it, I schedule a lot of things: Facebook posts, emails, text messages…it just makes giving that personal touch easier!

4. A group of like-minded entrepreneurs – this resource is a big middle of the cinnamon roll all by itself: support, encouragement, a group that will come to your events, people to bounce ideas off…people to help cheer you up and help you out of your salt flat…

5. Unroll.me – if you're anything like me, you've subscribed to an uncanny amount of emails. Clean it up with this simple to use app; in the spirit of de-cluttering!

6. Ok, one more…Headspace or Meditation apps – I personally have both. As an entrepreneur, you're pulled in a million directions and in the beginning, you're a one woman show. You need to find your balance and be centered. I find that in meditation. With the world, around us being so busy it's good to unplug at the end (or beginning) of the day and take some time for peace. You'll thank yourself. Namaste.

What makes you a woman that is making an impact?

I don't like to go on and on about myself but I do think that what makes me a woman that's making an impact is that I am genuine. What you see is what you get with me, always. Whether you're a client or a friend-I am just as passionate, love hard and am fiercely loyal. Today, I don't find a lot of people like me, so I hold onto them tight. I think that my impact will be felt because I am honest. I'm different. I think I can resonate with a lot of different people from all walks of life and I really try to walk my walk and be real.

Wild card question! Share whatever you would like the women reading your story to know about you, your business, or your journey.

Being real is something you don't often find in the fashion industry. After living abroad and coming back to the states, I realized that our culture is different from others. Our values are skewed at times. I carry lessons and values that I gathered while living in Mexico, from my international friends, and I try to live everyday as if it were my last.

Here are some fun facts about me:

- I grew up on welfare by a single mother. For most of my life, we didn't have money
- I've been homeless on several occasions.
- My work ethic is sick. I am writing this chapter on January 1st, 2017 while my husband and son are at a get together at our best friend's house.
- I speak fluent Spanish (hello bonus target market!)
- My husband is a police officer; he works overnight and we only see each other the equivalent of 2 days a week.
- In the last quarter of 2016, not only did I double my Style Box subscribers, but I got named in the Dallas shopping guide on Stay.com. I got hired as Creative Coordinator for Hope for Women magazine, and was also featured in a local magazine. You never know when your break is going to come!

Best of luck with your business – I wish you all the success in the world! I hope reading this has helped you be motivated and uplifted. You can find me online: www.mynimage.com and www.mynstylebox.com

Facebook + Instagram: MYN Image / MYN StyleBox

Learn more about Myaann Payne

Starting with her alter ego Miss Upside Down who donned her mother's sunglasses upside down along with her boots and shirts at three years old, fashion has always been a part of Myaann's life; serving others has always been her first passion.

In being a fashion and image consultant, she is able to marry her passion for helping people with her love of fashion. Myaann is originally from the Dallas Fort Worth metroplex, but has lived in Los Angeles and Mexico, developing a unique understanding for art, cultures, and different styles. She prides herself on being able to dress every body type, and always keeps her client's lifestyle and personal tastes in mind when dressing them. Along with personal wardrobe styling services, she has launched MYN Style Box, a subscription box service offering clients a unique personal shopper experience!

Website: www.mynimage.com

LESLIE ZANN

International Speaker, Trainer
and Sales Coach

Tell us a little about yourself. We want to learn about the person behind the brand.

I guess you could say I'm a self-made entrepreneur who has experienced success and failure, persevered through personal loss and heartache, and risen from the ashes – quite literally – to find her true purpose.

A long time ago, in the mid-1980s, I was married to my first husband, an architect, and we followed our dream of building homes. I went to night school to learn a little about building, then got my real estate license, and we were off and running. For about ten years we built high-end spec homes and grew a successful business with a full crew of employees, until we ran into something that happens frequently in California: a water moratorium. During a drought, the county put a stop to all new development. That forced us to move our business and our lives from the south to the north, into a very rural area of Northern California.

We sold everything we had, then spent half a million dollars on two lots in a golf course community. I hung my real estate license at the local ReMax office. We were prepared to start all over again, and in fact had invested heavily in that new start when the Realtor who had sold us the land called us months after the close of escrow and told us something that was getting too familiar: *"they enacted a water moratorium."* Yikes! How could this happen again?

To make a long and anxious story short, my husband ended up

working an hourly wage job at a Home Depot, and I started doing open houses all day, every night, and every weekend, to create some business. We were desperately trying to reduce our growing debt. Then one day I was at lunch with my real estate partner, and the hostess came running over to our table. "Leslie!" she cried out, "We just got a call from your office. Your house is burning down!"

Soon I'm driving up the hill, almost blinded by tears, slowed down by this open-bed truck creeping ahead of me, with hay blowing against the windshield. I'll never forget that hay in my face. All I could think about was our two dogs and my cat. As it turned out, the neighbors rescued our dogs, and my cat Tiffany was smart enough to hide out in a bathtub until a fireman found and revived her with an infant oxygen mask. I am not making that up; who could make that up? The revival of Tiffany was the front-page story in our small-town newspaper the next day!

But the worst was yet to come. Soon we learned we were under-insured, and eventually we were forced to declare bankruptcy. It was by far the worst experience of my life (although living in a dumpy motel for a while made a bad situation worse).

Not surprisingly, all the stress resulted in my gaining quite a bit of weight. Well, stress and what my mom called my "Corona-Dorito diet." (Yes ... that was my 'go-to under pressure' fuel.) Hah! Mom came to visit her bankrupt daughter. She took one look at me and my predicament, and uttered the words that would begin the turnaround of my life:

"Leslie, the only thing you can control is your health."

That single remark eventually led me into my mom's direct selling business for nutrition products which resulted not only in my losing thirty pounds, but over time I became a top leader in the company. Within two years, our financial picture improved dramatically; our marriage, however, did not survive the many challenges.

I continued to work in the direct selling profession for more than two decades, both independently and in corporate environments. I was inspired to make a difference, worked long hours and was on the road quite a bit. I was chasing a professional dream, and yet, I unintentionally lost the balance in my life. When my second marriage ended after fifteen years, I faced a deep crisis of motivation and direction that transformed me as a woman and ultimately resulted in the most successful work I have ever done.

Share with us what your business is and why you wanted to start this business.

Today I am a motivational speaker, author, trainer, and business coach. When I say I'm "self-made," I'm not kidding; I even made up my last name "Zann" and legalized it. Leslie Zann Consulting has been going strong since 2012, and these days I'm heavily booked with both new and repeat clients. In my profession, the greatest compliment is repeat business and referrals. I am fortunate that my business continues to be driven by both.

I was motivated to start Leslie Zann Consulting because I wanted to train, coach, motivate and inspire on my terms without the restrictions of a corporate template. In addition, I know what it's like to be at the absolute bottom. I know how easy it can be to lose focus and become emotionally defeated, making it much more difficult to recover. As I was inspired by others along my own personal journey now I'm focused on making a difference as a motivator for others.

I've always been a sales-oriented businessperson, and I learned the hard way that you can learn to respond to adversity on your terms. The ability to create a vision you can believe in, maintain respect for yourself, even when you feel challenged, and keep moving forward defines us as a person. I want everyone I encounter to understand that even the worst failure or set-back can be a step forward if you choose to look at it that way and then act with intention.

What have you learned about yourself in running your business?

I continue to learn, grow and evolve. If I had to narrow it down to my top three lessons, they would be:

1) My willingness to tackle new projects, learn new things, and collaborate;
2) My total commitment to discipline and time management; and
3) My understanding that success in business rests on a foundation of ongoing personal development.

My willingness to tackle new projects, learn new things, and collaborate:

This mindset has proven extremely valuable for me. Just because I've never done something before doesn't mean I can't learn how to do it well, or that I won't be great at it!

This liberates me to collaborate, rather than try to do everything myself. I have surrounded myself with excellent, skilled collaborators and assistants who are committed to my dream. I learn from them, and realize that I don't have to be the expert. I take all their smart advice, digest it, and decide how I choose to move forward. And then I act!

My total commitment to discipline and time management:

I firmly believe that many salespeople don't reach the level of success they desire because of a lack of accountability. When you are an employee, you become accustomed to someone else holding you accountable for your performance. When you embark on a new business as an entrepreneur, it's easy to get lost and avoid the actions that are in your best interest to take.

My total commitment to discipline and time management keeps me focused on the task at hand. I learned the value of taking consistent action in the key areas of my business, which has enabled me to build at an extraordinary pace, stretching even my own high standards for accountability.

My understanding that success in business rests on a foundation of ongoing personal development:

As I began my sales career, my mentors insisted I embrace personal development. I'm happy I took their advice. For the first time, I became aware of my thoughts and my ability to direct them. I suddenly understood that *what I think about, I bring about*, and this empowered me to design my life. I realized I could transform any area of my life, including my sales career, by shifting my mindset through the power of personal development.

With more than two decades in sales, I've experienced many highs and lows of success. Yes, there were difficult times when I could have focused on all the reasons why I should fail. But thanks to personal development, during those challenging times I could focus on all the reasons why I would persevere and create success. As those cycles ended, I found myself back on top. These experiences changed my perception of what I'm capable of and what's truly possible.

Personal development redefined me in every aspect of my life, not just in my career and business. Personal development was the catalyst for my evolution into the woman I am today and my continual growth.

Every day I continue to strengthen my commitment to not allow fears and limiting beliefs stop me from taking action. This commitment is not only the cornerstone of my own life, it is the cornerstone of the training I share with my clients.

What three things do you wish you would have known when you started?

Mindset **trumps** *skill set.* It's true that I believed this for years before I started my own business. Yet doing my vision work and seeing my vision manifest in this profoundly satisfying new business, regardless of the skill set I started with, has deepened my faith in this truth.

Success depends on self-development. My commitment to self-inquiry has created a sense of balance in my life. Not only can you include the search for meaning in your business life, it's key to success in the biggest sense. I tell my audiences that if they were only allowed to incorporate one piece of advice from our time together it would be their commitment to a daily personal development practice.

Good health is the foundation of everything. My commitment to a regular yoga practice set me on a path to prioritize physical fitness. I am stronger today than I was five years ago, and that's why I can work long hours at home, and travel frequently for speaking gigs, without burning out. My work/life balance has never been more in sync and it's reflected in everything I do.

My business is based on my commitment to share what I've learned in ways that are accessible and meaningful for others. One of my most popular programs is a 5-module online course called *Master Your Mindset: Your Breakthrough to Infinite Potential*. It takes you on a journey to discover your true capabilities, by harnessing the power of your mindset to believe in yourself and bring your vision to life. This is a game-changer for so many.

What 3 characteristics describe what has made you successful and why?

1) I'm service-driven. I always do my best for others, and that's what serves me best. Every day I ask myself how I can contribute to my clients' success. Too often salespeople use high-pressure tactics to achieve their goals, rather than focusing on the needs of the customer. Genuine interest in people and the issues they face is what separates a great salesperson from a mediocre one. A great salesperson excels at retaining customers and getting referrals – two key aspects of any successful business.

2) I'm honest and vulnerable. I don't pretend that I'm invincible or tough. I just tell the truth as I see it. I don't pretend to be perfect or to have always made the best choices. I recall and share my own difficult experiences, because I know that honesty about the challenges I've faced is inspirational to others in similar circumstances.

3) I deliver on my promises, and I'm always prepared to deliver more. We've all dealt with salespeople who tell you what you want to hear – but then can't deliver. It's always better to be honest about what you can and can't do and how quickly you can do it. When possible, top off your services with a little something extra and unexpected.

How have you defined your voice in your market?

I was fortunate to have developed a strong voice while working with my own direct selling team, and I've honed it while working for direct selling companies. Now I'm diversifying to talk about the secrets of motivation for all kinds of entrepreneurs, the self-employed, and self-starters of every description. It's very inspiring.

I believe strongly in delivering a valuable message with an authentic voice. Additionally, I believe that everyone can achieve outrageous results with the right mindset, a heavy dose of gratitude and consistent action.

I have defined myself as someone who has overcome adversity and is now designing the life of her dreams every day. I believe this is possible for everyone.

What would you advise someone who is struggling with building their brand?

First there are the brand-building basics that apply to every business situation: Deliver what you promise when you promise to deliver it. Offer excellent customer service. If someone is unhappy with your work, figure out a way to make them happy. Get the staff support you need to do the work your clients expect.

Authenticity and integrity are the two most important factors in building a strong personal brand. When people learn, they can count on you to deal with them honestly – that you put their needs first – you build a personal brand that your clients want to share with others. Remember that word-of-mouth is what makes – or breaks – your brand.

When you are your brand, as I am, my other recommendation is to find good mentors: one for your business, one for your mindset, and one for your lifestyle.

None of these must be a lifetime commitment, but each should be highly targeted to focus on your next step. In business, for example, watch for someone who has already done what you want to do next in your business. For your mindset, look for someone whose self-awareness and style of communicating impresses you. For your lifestyle, you may want a yoga teacher, sports coach, or nutrition counselor, depending on what your next step might be.

In any part of your search, don't be afraid to ask for help! It's amazing how effective it is to simply state your needs out loud to someone. Even if that person can't help you directly, often they will later meet someone who can, think of you, and put you in touch. I've even made incredible contacts by announcing my next business goal to a packed audience. Whenever I feel compelled to do that, my first intention is to motivate them to dream bigger, but I also know there could be someone sitting in that audience who is ready and willing to collaborate with me to our mutual benefit.

Staying motivated when things don't seem to be coming together is a challenge at times. How do you motivate yourself? What would you advise someone else?

I depend on my daily personal development practice as my model for success. No one can prevent me from meditating, from practicing yoga, staying in shape, or from reading for wisdom and inspiration. These are my at-home priorities at which I can always succeed, and that sets the pace for what I do in business.

This overall practice helps me turn fear into faith, and disappointment into innovation. When something happens that I would prefer not to have happen, or when I was expecting a different outcome, I am quick to let go of my preferences and expectations. Instead of complaining, resenting, or expecting the worst, I can feel curiosity about how this latest unfavorable event might lead to a better opportunity or result than I had imagined.

Additionally, I focus on the vision I've created for my business. I have a very clear and compelling vision that I refine on a regular basis. Having clarity on what I choose to create is a driver for me. It drives my discipline, my actions and my courage. Having a clear, compelling vision coupled with my personal development practice allows me to not only stay motivated but to raise my motivation level to new heights!

What has been your most effective marketing tool / strategy and why?

The most effective marketing strategy is to meet your clients and prospects where they are. Once you have found them, speak to them authentically. Believe in your own message, and have faith in your own abilities. This is why your mindset is so important. If you don't believe in yourself, it will be difficult to convince others that they should believe in you.

Speaking and training is still my most effective way to connect with new people. I am very blessed that my business is driven by repeat business and referrals, two indicators that I am making a difference in my clients' lives and bottom line.

Social media has been an important channel for keeping in touch with my audience between live events and for growing my prospect database. My Facebook following is very robust, and I am also active on Twitter and Instagram.

No matter what channel you use for marketing, a genuine message delivered to the right audience is the best marketing strategy.

One of the biggest struggles women entrepreneurs have is how to price themselves. What advice would you share about pricing your services and offerings?

Find out what other people in your profession are charging and start there. Stand strong in the value of what you provide. Never give your best services away for free. In many businesses, it is useful to offer get-to-know-me products or occasional discounts and economical packaging of products or services, but that is very different from working for free. From day one I remembered a piece of wisdom from a very successful entrepreneur who said, "Wealth is created when you bring value to the market place." My intention is always to bring high value to everything I do.

I ask for feedback, and I listen to all of it. People often have suggestions for improvement I can act on to offer better products and services. Plus, positive feedback is equally important. While it may be tempting to focus only on the criticisms, it's the positive feedback that validates and encourages me. It bolsters my belief in myself, my business and the value of my products. I make a point to take in all the positive feedback through my 'gratitude' filter rather than my 'ego' filter. This keeps me humble and focused on service.

What advice would you give to a woman entrepreneur who is ready to take her business to the next level?

Besides finding good mentors and collaborators, as I've mentioned, an all-important step is creating and refining your vision. Vision is not just wishful thinking, hoping for the best, or waiting for your imagination to be fulfilled. It's a disciplined approach to envisioning what you can and want to be, and then planning the steps that will take you there.

Sometimes your initial plans won't work out, so you must learn the skills of adapting on the fly, staying aware that while your *route* may change, you are still moving in the direction of your ultimate vision. That vision should be about all-around success, your maximum fulfillment as a human being, not just a goal expressed in dollars, achievements, or rewards.

I am so keen on vision work that at lesliezann.com my online gift for new members of my ZannFan community is a multi-media program entitled *Ignite Your Vision*. One thing I know for sure: when it's time to ignite your passion for your life, there is no better way to do that than by creating, revisiting and/or enhancing your vision. You can design your life, and it's an exciting process.

What "must have" resources would you recommend someone use in their business?

- Personal Development Practice – Many entrepreneurs don't understand the power of personal development. They don't think they have time to spend working on themselves. "I'm too busy working on my business! I don't have time to work on myself!" Believe me, you don't have time to NOT work on yourself. It's YOUR vision and YOUR perseverance that will create a successful business. I guarantee that with personal development, you will save time, because every day you will clarify and re-affirm your vision and purpose, and will know how to focus your attention to move toward your goals.
- Quality assistant(s) doing the right support activities – Don't try to go it alone. Don't spend your time on activities anyone could do (such as basic customer service) or spinning your wheels on activities someone else could do better (such as graphic design or database management). Just because you can do it, doesn't mean you should.

- Time Management tools – Find the time management tools that work for you. That includes a calendar system that works for all areas of your life including your personal life; a project management system so you can stay on top of your client work; and business planning tools that allow you to map out your goals, marketing and finances.

What makes you a woman who is making an impact?

I can see the effect of my business in the success of my clients and customers. Every year, I see my coaching and speaking clients expand their revenue. I'm fortunate that my business creates measurable results that I get to see as I work with my clients' year after year!

I'm all about results! I humbly admit that I can effectively inspire and motivate my audience. That's important for sure. My larger intention is that they walk out the door, or complete a course or online program, and find their belief is expanded, their dream is broader, their path is clearer, and they take action like never before.

Although I work with many large, global companies, I find a lot of satisfaction working with start-up companies. It's a way of giving back that's especially gratifying.

My charitable work is a key driver for me. I am dedicated to making a difference for the causes that inspire me. I am so grateful for everything in my life and am driven to give back, to come from service and shine my light.

Wild card question! Share whatever you would like the women reading your story to know about you, your business, or your journey.

One of my friends says, "You have a heart for the population."

That means I care about my audience, their success, and their happiness. They can feel it because I'm authentic about wanting the best for them. That's because I'm not looking outside myself for my own success. My goals are to stay humble, transparent, vulnerable and joyful. I include a high dose of discipline too. I consistently focus on my own health and inner development because I know that's where my own success and joy is rooted. I can talk about my failures because I've seen how they led to my success, so I'm modeling that resilience and transformation for my audience.

I think my capacity to understand my audience combined with my deep commitment to show them how to keep walking forward; inspires their trust in me and opens them to my advice. When it works for them, when they see the results in both their personal life and their business success; they come back for more. Together we are moving towards our unlimited potential.

Learn more about Leslie Zann

Leslie Zann is a master at helping people recognize and discover their true and limitless potential. With more than two decades in the sales profession, Leslie has developed a unique talent for helping people overcome their potential-stopping "limiting beliefs".

Leslie is a sought-after international speaker, trainer and sales coach to top sales professionals. She challenges her clients to "be willing to see things differently." And in doing so, she challenges them to create unprecedented success with no limits.

Visit her at lesliezann.com and become a ZannFan. You'll receive a complimentary gift titled, Ignite Your Vision to help you craft a compelling vision for your business and your life!

Her Facebook site is a popular destination for sales people at facebook.com/lesliezannconsulting

DR. JANE TORRIE, DC

Wellness Consultant

Tell us a little about yourself. We want to learn about the person behind the brand.

I have done many things in my life most of which have pointed me directly or indirectly toward my passion of helping people experience optimal health and wellness. I've found often from a retrospective view that I can see how all of life's experiences from a "dead end job" to a course in college that I thought was useless are woven together to create the rich tapestry of life. I love living things and life. It is my passion to help others experience their richest and fullest life in terms of their wellness. I often tell people that just as water is in three phases: liquid, gas and solid, we humans are physical, emotional and spiritual. It is through these that we experience life.

I am the mother of two adult sons. They both make me very proud!

Share with us what your business is and why you wanted to start this business.

I am a Wellness Consultant focusing on chiropractic, nutrition and healthy fat loss. All my life experiences have converged to bring me to my current level of understanding and focus. My family background is in the helping and health fields. My parents were both clinical social workers, my sister is a medical doctor and my extended family includes teachers, MDs and a botanist!

It is in my blood to work with people to achieve optimal health on all levels. My perspective is to approach the physical body and bring in the emotional and spiritual when they are the appropriate approaches. I have worked as a chiropractor for over 30 years. At times, it was my primary work and sometimes it was "on the side." There was a period when I had to stop working as a chiropractor due to personal health issues. When I was well enough to be able to return to chiropractic practice, I knew that God was restoring my ability to use my gift of healing through chiropractic.

I have renewed my focus and business attention since then. I have included two additional businesses, one of which is a body sculpting business using LipoLight technology. A crucial part of my business is my Juice Plus franchise. It is adding an additional income stream as well as improving the health of my patients from the inside out and helping them to maintain their adjustments.

My practice is one in which people experience peace, love and the restoration of their God-given health and wellbeing.

What have you learned about yourself in running your business?

I have learned that having the gift of healing is the beginning of having a business, not the end! I have spent considerable time and attention in developing a business model that works for me. I have learned that practicing in a way that is congruous with my goals and ethics requires me to be willing to change my models and methods.

I've also learned that I can be my own biggest obstacle. Arguing with reality because I think things ought to be a certain way is counterproductive. Coming to the realization that I needed to move from billing health insurance to being a self-pay practice was a good example. I thought I had to do what "everyone else" was doing. When I finally switched from taking insurance to being self-pay, it improved my cash flow, freed up my time and didn't diminish my practice numbers.

What three things do you wish you would have known when you started?

- I'm not bound by others' models of what I should do.
- When I seek God for my purpose and direction and commit my plans and work to Him, He will open the doors for me.
- I need to trust my own, God-given intuition!

What 3 characteristics describe what has made you successful and why?

1. I have stayed true to my gifting and to functioning out of integrity.
2. Being bold and courageous in my adherence to my principles.
3. I started with what I had and have grown and developed as I move along.

When I operate in a way that is consistent with my values, then I can move past obstacles and see solutions to situations that seem impossible.

How have you defined your voice in your market?

I use many chiropractic techniques and meld them into my own style. I incorporate lifestyle and nutrition to help people understand how they can actively reclaim their own health. When that happens, they can see how to take responsibility for their own health. When people shift from seeing me and other health care providers as dispensing health to them, to seeing themselves as empowered to live in the fullness of their divine destiny, we can truly partner in achieving optimal health. My voice may not be the loudest nor my business the largest but for those who come to my office, the experience is a unique and empowering one.

What would you advise someone who is struggling with building their brand?

The primary thing is to be sure that you are aligned with the plan and the destiny that God has for you! When you are aligned, the doors will open before you.

Have your mission written down and firmly in mind; make your decisions based upon that mission!

Staying motivated when things don't seem to be coming together is a challenge at times. How do you motivate yourself? What would you advise someone else?

For me, the best advice I have ever received is regarding moving forward. It is "When you don't know what to do, do what you know to do!" This advice has served me well both in business and my personal life!

Discouragement is always lurking and waiting to pull us down into mediocrity. Sinking into that doesn't serve us but moving forward, even when we think we don't know what we are doing is key! I motivate myself by staying plugged in with God's perspective. That means reading and listening to messages from those who are set free in the LORD. I've also made key alignments with other chiropractors, health coaches and those who promote a grassroots movement of people taking full responsibility for their own health. I am not operating on my own but in alliance with like-minded people.

What has been your most effective marketing tool / strategy and why?

My most effective marketing strategy is word of mouth referrals and Google reviews. I must remember to ask people to write a Google review. I answer everyone. Paying for advertising in print, on Facebook and at sporting events has not worked well for me.

One of the biggest struggles women entrepreneurs have is how to price themselves. What advice would you share about pricing your services and offerings?

I certainly want to nurture and care for others by giving deals or discounts. What I've learned is that if I undervalue my services, others will do the same thing. My services are priced comparably to others in my area. Calling around to other businesses is how I have done that.

What advice would you give to a woman entrepreneur who is ready to take her business to the next level?

Taking business to the next level requires looking at the current season as a harvest season. If you were a farmer, when harvest season comes, you work long hard hours to bring in the harvest. When you are developing a new business, or shifting to a higher level, be prepared to be out of balance for a time and pour yourself into that time. It is worth it!

What "must have" resources would you recommend someone use in their business?

Coaching from mentors in your field is critical. Coaching can come in the form of books, seminars, CDs or one on one coaching. I have benefited from all the above methods. Reading *Go Pro* by Eric Worre, *Success Magazine*, *Take the Stairs* by Rory Vaden, and *Switch on Your Brain* by Dr. Caroline Leaf are books that have really impacted me. Listening to Jim Rohn CDs is another great resource. With my Juice Plus business, we have many opportunities for personal development. Personal development is useful in all areas of life from business to personal!

Another resource that I find invaluable is called Emotional Freedom Technique (EFT) or Tapping. It helps the brain to update old decisions that have become filters through which we view the world and make our decisions. If I am viewing the world through "no one values me," for example, it makes me hit a brick wall repeatedly when I try to advance. Clearing that out using EFT allows me to walk more freely in my true destiny.

What makes you a woman that is making an impact?

I am making an impact because I am doing what I was gifted to do. I don't stop learning. I am barely five feet tall, weigh more than I should and am 65 years old. More than one of my loyal patients has walked into my office and thought, "how can she do what I need done?" I treat patients from newborns to 80+ year olds. I treat male and female, tiny to over 300 pounds. In my own power, I would be unable to do all of this. In my gifting, I can do this on a regular basis. This is my impact!

Wild card question! Share whatever you would like the women reading your story to know about you, your business, or your journey.

I believe the most important thing that I can impart is how critical it is to walk in the power and authority which God has placed within you. When I am not walking in that power and authority, it is an indication that I am operating in self-limiting beliefs that are at odds with my conscious desire. That is called cognitive dissonance and, if unchecked, it will cause me to manifest my limiting belief, not my conscious desire. There is intense internal warfare. When that warfare occurs, if I pursue it, it will lead me into greater authority as I update my unconscious belief. It is through that activity that I advance, accelerate and elevate!

Learn more about Dr. Jane Torrie, DC

 Dr. Jane has worn many hats in her life. She has sold donuts, waitressed and been the church and school secretary for a Christian outreach.

Her love of learning and understanding the subtleties of our elegant bodies led to her independent studies of herbology and nutrition and, eventually, to her BS in Human Biology and Doctor of Chiropractic degree. That is where she truly found her passion and destiny. On that journey, she has committed to being an entrepreneur in the field of health and wellness. She is living her overarching mission of helping people experience optimal health and wellness.

Website: www.DrJaneTorrie.com

LISA PULLIAM

Speaker and Author

Tell us a little about yourself. We want to learn about the person behind the brand.

For those of you reading this book, I pray my words and stories will bring you peace, joy and inspiration. I was born into a large, tight-knit, immigrant family that, like many, came to this country with dreams for a better life. Not a day goes by that I do not think about my great grandparents and desire to emulate their faith, love and ambition in my life. My husband Chris and I just celebrated 25 years of marriage in the magnificent tropical paradise of Punta Cana, Dominican Republic. The Lord has blessed us with four beautiful children, an incredible son-in-law, and our first grandbaby on the way. Chris is the Senior Minister of a church in Texas, so that makes me a minister's wife (or as they say in some churches, a "First Lady") which has a whole set of responsibilities in and of itself. In Punta Cana, where the water is a brilliant turquoise blue, more than any swimming pool I have ever swam in, and the sand feels like sugar and butter between my toes, I saw this inscription painted on the side of the catamaran:

"When was the last time you did something for the FIRST time?"

Last week, on that very day, Chris surprised me with an afternoon of parasailing and snuba-diving for the very first time! Snuba is a cross between scuba diving and snorkeling. It is a mask with an oxygen hose attached to a mouthpiece which allows the participant to dive ten to twenty feet below the surface of this breathtaking oversized aquarium. WOW is all I can say! It was a day I will never forget.

Share with us what your business is and why you wanted to start this business.

About seven years ago, I was eager to launch into a career after raising children as a stay at home mom or "domestic engineer" for fifteen years. Part of my motivation was financial. Our children were hitting those teenage years, and we knew another stream of income was necessary to navigate the waters of the oncoming decade or so. The other reason was my desire to step out in faith into a new season of my life.

I have always had an entrepreneurial spirit. When my great grandparents immigrated to the United States in 1902, they worked hard to establish a life for themselves. They started businesses and became successful in this new country. So, through much prayer, seeking and exploring several different career paths, I sensed His voice leading me to start my own business. I found a great fit in the direct sales industry with a new company called Ambit Energy, a retail energy provider marketing electricity and natural gas services in the deregulated markets around the country.

What have you learned about yourself in running your business?

When I became my own boss and the CEO of my company, I quickly realized that the number one person I was accountable to was me. The number one income earner of my company has often said, "If you want to know the reason for your success and the reason for your failure, just look in the mirror." I learned that there was nobody else to blame or to wait on. I learned if success was meant to be, it was up to me. This was a tough lesson to learn at times, but such a growing experience.

One of my greatest strengths is that I am a people person. Though I believe all personality types can be successful in direct sales as long if they are willing to grow and develop themselves personally, being a people person helped me get started with confidence. I have learned that I enjoy speaking, training, and empowering others to be successful. The people side of my business has been a blast!

I have also learned that the detail, task oriented side of business is not my favorite part. Administrative activities, tracking daily calls and follow ups, finances and budget activities, etc. are a challenge for me. I have learned ways of getting the job done but those ways are not the most fulfilling aspects of running a business! Get me to the weekly business presentation, the training, the one-on-one coffee, or lunch appointment, and I am in my element!

One more thing I learned: I can take a LOT more "no's" than I thought I could! Hearing the word, "No" can be difficult to overcome, but once I decided to stop taking the "no's" personally, my business began to take off!

What three things do you wish you would have known when you started?

1. Not everyone will want to be a customer or will join me in business! In fact, some of my closest friends and family who I knew would say Yes, said No!

2. Some simple, organizational skills and techniques would have been great. I had been raising children for fifteen years. I could read to toddlers, nurse a baby, cook dinner, and clean a toilet all at the same time! But when it came to business, I lacked personal organizational skills.

3. Drawing boundaries between personal, family and business time is CRITICAL. For a few years, I allowed these to run together. My family, though supportive, suffered at times because I lacked this discerning skill. Creating balance in life is essential for a truly happy, fulfilled, relationship-rich life. This is a daily challenge.

What 3 characteristics (describe) have made you successful and why?

1. Tenacity: some call it stubbornness (as my mom did when I was young!), but when I have a strong desire to accomplish something, I will figure out a way to get it done. I have learned to not let the dream stealers of the world take my dream and my goal away from me. I am an ambitious woman.

2. Humility: I understand I can learn from other leaders who have had the success I desire. Early on in my business, I became a sponge for knowledge, wisdom, and experience from others whom I admire. I ask a lot of questions, read books on personal growth and development, and spend time with leaders as often as I am able. I also enjoy webinars and training calls, always eagerly listening for nuggets of gold that I can implement in my business immediately.

3. Trust: I have heard Dr. John Maxwell say the strongest of leaders love their people. When a team knows their leader truly cares about them, trust emerges. Trust is the foundation of any great team. My team knows I love and care about them…and trust can move mountains.

How have you defined your voice in your market?

I have always enjoyed writing. As a teenager, I began learning how to journal my thoughts and prayers, and this became the way I processed all that was going on around me, good and bad, happy and sad. Out of my love for writing, my first book, *Toes in the Sand, My Journey from Domestic Engineer to Entrepreneur,* was born. My message to women is this: Take some time to dig deep into your heart and soul so you can discover who you were created to be. To find this time requires escaping your life for a few hours or even a few days if possible. Dig your toes in the sand (or wherever your happy place is). My happy place happens to be surrounded by sand, sun, palm trees, and beautiful water. I feel closest to God near the ocean. Sometimes when I only have a few hours to spend, I escape to a local winery and sit outside on a beautiful day. I encourage you to find your "happy place", a place where you can feel energy, peace, and joy. Be INSPIRED. Grab a blank journal or notebook and start writing. Dig deep and consider these questions:

What do you like and enjoy about your life right now? List everything for which you are grateful.

- Where do you see yourself in two, five or ten years? Describe your life and yourself relationally, financially, spiritually, emotionally, health and fitness. WHAT DOES YOUR IDEAL LIFE LOOK LIKE? How will you feel when you are living this life?
- What are your fears, your insecurities, your strengths, your hopes, and your goals, your dreams? Write everything down that comes to your mind. Let your thoughts and desires flow onto the paper.
- Do you have mentors and balcony people in your life, people who will cheer you on? If not, seek them out.
- Are there people who tear you down and discourage you from pursuing your dreams? Pray for them. Most of all, be cautious with whom you share your goals.

Then take your shaky, first step. Then the next day, take another. Then another, and then another.

You can visit my website at www.lisacarolpulliam.com and go to my Reflections section for a detailed outline of this exercise. It's called "Dig Deep and Find the Treasure in You."

What would you advise someone who is struggling with building their brand?

I have been in the process of branding myself for a while, and I am still on the road of this "branding journey". What is most important is to know who you are, what motivates and inspires you, what your message is, and who your audience is. Ask yourself these significant questions when you have some alone time in your happy place. For in-depth assistance and support in developing your brand, find a business coach for entrepreneurial women and allow someone with expertise in the area of branding and marketing to guide you in this process.

Staying motivated when things don't seem to be coming together is a challenge at times. How do you motivate yourself? What would you advise someone else?

Though I am a "people person", I find true motivation in spending time with God, listening to uplifting music, and journaling my thoughts and prayers. I absolutely love being around the water, whether it's a lake, the ocean, or a beautiful backyard pool. Through a recent 40 Day Prayer Challenge, I learned to be very specific with my prayers, hopes, dreams and even my frustrations and discouragements. God knows exactly what's on our heart, and He longs to give us the desires that lie within. So be specific.

I also enjoy walking, listening to motivational music, and when I can take the time, "escaping" to a local family-owned winery in East Texas called Kiepersol where I enjoy sipping my favorite glass of red wine while overlooking the magnificent vineyards. If you are ever in East Texas, call me and we will spend an afternoon there!

What has been your most effective marketing tool / strategy and why?

My business is built through personal relationship marketing. Therefore, I have concentrated my growth and development on learning interpersonal skills. Several years ago, I helped start a new BNI (Business Networking International) chapter in my hometown and through this weekly meeting, I learned the valuable skills of networking with other professionals and how to provide quality referrals to them. I found the more I learned to help others grow their businesses, the more mine grew! I joined a Toastmasters Club to improve my speaking and communication skills. I have attended several conferences, and read many books that teach and train on developing people skills: how to meet someone new, build a relationship, make a contact, and how to make an effective phone call asking someone to look at my business or try my service. Learning how to connect with people is the single most important skill you need to develop to build a successful business.

What advice would you give to a woman entrepreneur who is ready to take her business to the next level?

Find a mentor or business coach. I cannot overemphasize the significance of having successful women in your life, pouring into you with your best interest in mind. I have several mentors and a business coach who are invaluable to me. They encourage me toward my goals, and sometimes they give me a swift kick in the pants when I am off track! Remember when I said early in this chapter that the number one person I am accountable to is me? That is true.

However, I have discovered the value in having someone else help to hold me accountable. I remember last year when I set a goal to go walking at 6 am daily before my children woke up. I had tried and tried to implement this daily discipline with little success and not much consistency. One day, I called a friend in the neighborhood and asked her if she would like to join me for my morning walk. She agreed, and we began a consistent daily regimen that lasted for months until the weather got too cold to continue! Trust me, many mornings I wanted to push snooze and go back to sleep, but I knew Lesley and her dog Penny would be waiting for me, so up and out I went!

What "must have" resources would you recommend someone use in their business?

Being an entrepreneur can be a tough road at times. The highs can be high and the lows are low. I discovered very quickly I needed to be cautious and intentional about what was feeding my mind. Whether you are an avid reader or not, I encourage you to find positive, motivational material to sink your teeth into daily. Every morning I start my day with prayer, a daily devotional, and meditation on God's plan for me, my life, my family and my business. Then I listen to 3-5 minutes of daily success teaching from Darren Hardy, called "Darren's Daily". I also receive and listen to "A Minute with Maxwell" with Dr. John Maxwell.

The nuggets of wisdom I gain from these tools give me actionable ideas I can implement in my business. My business coach, Amy Applebaum, interviews successful entrepreneurial women on her coaching calls. When I go for my morning walk, I listen to these call recordings, as well as audio of Jim Rohn and other great leaders of all time. I call this being "plugged in." Just like the electricity that runs into your home powering your hair dryer, coffee pot, and TV, you must plug in to sources that give you the positive energy you need to keep focused on the goals and dreams of your heart.

What makes you a woman that is making an impact?

Along my journey of motherhood and entrepreneurship, I decided what matters most in life is not what everyone thinks of me. Life is not about impressing others with fancy cars, things, stuff, or the world's view of success. What matters most in life is being true to the woman God has called me to be. What matters most to me is having the respect of those closest to me: my God, my spouse, my children, my close family and friends. Being a woman who is making an impact means being free to be all God has created me to be: fun, silly, adventuresome, genuine, kind, encouraging, and inspiring to everyone whose path I cross.

Wild card question! Share whatever you would like the women reading your story to know about you, your business, or your journey.

When I was sixteen years old, I returned from a Young Life Camp in Colorado held in the summer. I was asked to share my life-changing story at a Young Life banquet a couple months later in front of 500 parents and ministry supporters. Through that speech, the Lord planted a seed inside me to inspire others through public speaking. As I grew in business, I was reminded how much I enjoy speaking, teaching and training groups of people and inspiring them to be successful. I had the awe-inspiring moment to speak at our company's national conference in front of 3,000 people (every bit as exhilarating as a parasailing 100 feet above the ocean and snuba diving with the swordfish)! I have a desire and a passion to speak to women's ministry groups and business networking groups and inspire women everywhere to face their fears, and step into the life God has created them to live.

I welcome calls and emails from you!
My contact info is (903) 830-5303
Email: lisacarolpulliam@gmail.com
Website: www.lisacarolpulliam.com

Learn more about Lisa Pulliam

 After sixteen years of juggling responsibilities of stay-at-home mom of four children and pastor's wife, Lisa knew it was time to launch her own career. Lisa found a great fit in the direct sales industry and achieved the leadership level of Executive Consultant during her fourth year with her company. Lisa's first book, Toes in the Sand is her journey from pastor's wife and stay at home mom of four children into, entrepreneurship. She has enjoyed her leap of faith is passionate about inspiring women to step into the life they were created to live.

Website: www.lisacarolpulliam.com

CHARMAINE MARSHALL

Fashion Stylist and Personal Shopper

Tell us a little about yourself. We want to learn about the person behind the brand.

I am a lover of fashion, all things artistic and creative. Ever since I was a little girl I have always been in love with fashion. So much so I would save my allowance to buy the latest fashion magazines. I studied these magazines. I knew who all the models were, all the fashion designers, and all the makeup artists. As I got older and started working I could start seeing the clothing of these designers in person at the companies I was working for. I studied their design, sewing techniques and how they used fabric.

This has been over a 20-year obsession with fashion. I have had the honor and privilege of working with some of the best luxury brand companies such as Neiman Marcus, Saks Fifth Avenue, and Tiffany & Co. just to name a few. At Tiffany and Co. came my love of jewelry and jewelry design. Hence my creative juices were flowing and I began my jewelry collection. As time went on I wanted to encompass my love of fashion with my personal shopping and wardrobe styling services. So, I incorporated that in to the business that I now have today which is Charmaine Marshall Designs.

Share with us what your business is and why you wanted to start this business.

The name of my business is Charmaine Marshall Designs. It is a multi-faceted company that includes personal shopping, wardrobe styling and jewelry design. I have always loved, creating things and making individuals feel and look their best. I find that I am the most at peace when I am in my creative mode.

I wanted to start the business because of my love of fashion and being able to offer my expertise through my craft of designing jewelry and styling clients. It is the perfect extension of oneself to add that last element to an outfit - that final touch.

What have you learned about yourself in running your business?

I have learned that whatever I set my mind to do I can do it. Running a business is hard work and I must keep pushing myself to be motivated and striving for excellence. I must do what I have to do now to be successful so later I can do what I want to do. So, one day I will have others working for me so I will still have to work hard but not as hard. That is the goal.

What three things do you wish you would have known when you started?

The three things that I wish I would have known when I started was that I am only one person. To be successful one needs to have a support system to help propel them forward with their business goals. I was so dependent on doing everything myself. So, I asked family and friends to help me and that allowed me to progress a lot faster with my business goals.

Secondly, I wish I would have been a lot more thorough with my business plans. To produce the results, you want for your business you need to stick closely to your plans. I needed to make sure that I was looking at my business plans monthly to stay on track.

Lastly, make sure to shop for the best prices on business cards and to have plenty on hand. You do not have to have the most expensive business card to make an impression. Companies such as VistaPrint have the heavy card stock that some of the more expensive business card companies have at a fraction of the price.

What 3 characteristics describe what has made you successful and why?

The three things that have made me successful are my drive, determination and faith. My drive has propelled me to reach some of my goals that I have set out for myself and for my business. The determination that I possess comes from wanting to show my daughters that anything you put your mind to can be done successfully. My faith comes from believing in myself when others do not. Also, that God always has a plan for us, we just must be patient and believe. Knowing that good things will come my way if I continue to work hard for what I want to accomplish with my business.

How have you defined your voice in your market?

I have defined my voice in my market by networking, doing speaking engagements, collaborations with designers, staying in contact with my clients and employers from my past experiences and by asking for referrals from my clients. I also use social media to promote my business and stay in contact with my followers.

Stay motivated when things don't seem to be coming together is a challenge at times. How do you motivate yourself? What would you advise someone else?

I stay motivate by my family, and the positive people I have in my life that truly believe in me and my passions. I avoid negativity, stay focused and positive. I surround myself with what I want to become and emulate.

What would you advise someone who is struggling with building their brand?

I would advise them to get a business coach. It is one of the best things that I have done for my business. I have gotten clarity as to what I should be focusing on, how to be profitable, what goals I should set for a month, a year and 5 years from now. It has helped me to be able to stay in line with my business plans and become more successful. Thanks Kimberly Pitts!

What has been your most effective marketing tool / strategy and why?

My most effective marketing tool is social media. It allows me to interact with my clients, keep them updated on the latest product launches, promotions and just allows them to see what is going on with my brand. It also keeps me in the forefront of their mind if they should need your services. I have a lot of clients that I have picked up just from my social media accounts.

One of the biggest struggles women entrepreneurs have is how to price themselves. What advice would you share about pricing your services and offerings?

The advice I would give about pricing is not to underestimate your worth. Show that your brand has value. Do your research on how others in your field are pricing and know your market. Be confident when asked how much your services are and stick to it. If they ask for a discount be confident in saying no. It is alright to say no. As the saying goes as one doors closes another door opens. By sticking to your pricing, you are not diluting your brand and staying true to yourself.

What advice would you give to a woman entrepreneur who is ready to take her business to the next level?

I would advise a women entrepreneur who is ready to take her business to the next level to have all her i's dotted and all her t's crossed. Make sure to have all your business processes and procedures in place. Look at the team you have surrounded yourself with thus far. Make sure they are what you need on this next level you are going to. If not, adjust accordingly. Make sure you have your business legal game on point. Meaning make sure to have your company incorporated properly to protect yourself and your business. And congratulations on your next level move, you go girl!

What "must have" resources would you recommend someone use in their business?

The "must have" resources that I would recommend to someone to use in their business is to always have a support system in place. Your support system should include a motivator. This is your go to person that you become accountable to that will push you to meet your goals and accomplish your dreams. This can be a business coach such as Kimberly Pitts of UImpact.

Also, included in your support system a tech guru; someone that you can turn to for social media questions, someone that can help implement processes and procedures to help your company run smoothly and efficiently. Lastly, include a wardrobe consultant/fashion stylist to help you represent your brand fashionably and stylishly which will help you to get your brand message across.

What makes you a woman that is making an impact?

What makes me a woman that is making an impact is that I am serving as a role model for other entrepreneurs showing them that whatever your passion or dreams are you too can accomplish your businesses goals and dreams as long you have faith in yourself. You flourish by living life daily as a success in your mind and owning that.

Wild card question! Share whatever you would like the women reading your story to know about you, your business, or your journey.

If you have any questions, please let me know and I will be more than happy to answer any questions you have.

For all of you ladies and gentlemen that are looking to define your fashion sense to be more in line with your brand, Charmaine Marshall Designs offers a full range of service from personal shopping, closet cleanses, wardrobe styling for speaking engagements, special occasions, wardrobe at a glance (a weekly or monthly service that puts all your outfits together for you.) creative direction for photo shoots that brands individuals and/or products. This service includes the photographer, hair and makeup artist, and wardrobe styling.

Please visit our website at www.charmainemarshall.com or message us at info@charmainemarshall.com for more information on our services.

It was such an honor and privilege to be a part of UImpact Publishing, Behind Her Brand Series Volume 6. Thank you, ladies,

- Kim, Adorah and Mandy for putting this together for us and for all your support.

Learn more about Charmaine Marshall

Dallas based in demand fashion stylist, and personal shopper Charmaine Marshall is turning heads with her own bold and daring collection of jewelry designs. This "wearable" art is anything but understated. Her handcrafted designs draw on the colors and textures of nature. While her one of a kind pieces evoke images of trophies taken on safari or artifacts from an expedition, Charmaine's designs convey a strength and polished beauty that stands out in settings from national fashion magazine editorials to star studded celebrity affairs.

Her discerning eye comes from her 20 years of extensive industry background, which include certification in diamonds and diamond grading from the Gemological Institute of America. And her expertise is complimented by years of customer service at leading retailers such Tiffany & Co., DeBeers Diamond Jewelers, Neiman Marcus and Saks Fifth Avenue.

Website: www.charmainemarshall.com

RUTHIE STAALSEN

DecRenew Interiors
Renowned Interior Designer

Tell us a little about yourself. We want to learn about the person behind the brand.

I was born in 1967 in South Africa and spent my childhood there. At the age of ten, my parents told my siblings and I that they felt called to leave South Africa to become missionaries. We watched our parents sell everything: our beautiful home, nice cars, and everyday luxuries we had grown so accustomed to, so they could take a leap of faith into the unknown. My sister, brother, and I embraced this new journey and started to get excited about what lied ahead. I'll never forget the goodbyes we had to say at the airport on the morning we left. Hugs were exchanged between the cousins we grew up with, as well as friends we loved dearly. Mom and dad told us that we were each only allowed to take one duffle bag with us. Once packed, each one was filled to the brim with a few of the things we loved dearly, but most of all, the things we needed. Waving goodbye to the stable life we knew as we went up the escalator is a memory I will never forget. Little did I know that our family of five adventure had only begun.

Although it was hard, we were fortunate enough to travel the world. Mexico, Guatemala, and Panama were only several of the places we spent time in. The privilege of being able to experience different cultures was the greatest gift I received from my childhood. We moved many times and had to say goodbye to old friends repeatedly, but we were always able to make new ones. My personal character was built by living in different lifestyles. I learned quickly to make the small things count, because life was not easy, especially since we lived in some primitive areas. We bathed and washed our clothes in local rivers, carried water long distances so we could boil and drink it, baked and cooked over open fires, lived in villages where we didn't speak the language, slept in hammocks in the middle of the jungle, and for fun--walked miles to our favorite waterfall. We became resilient to change and learned to go with the flow. My mom and dad were amazing in the way they knew how to make our house a home wherever we were. They surrounded us with the small things that made it feel cozy, but most of all, a love that we felt when we were all together. Our home was always filled with people because my parents were constantly entertaining. It was a refuge for us to create memories with these new friends that soon became our adopted family.

When I was a freshman in high school, my parent's job was reassigned to Texas, where I went to school and graduated. The day after my graduation, my parents got a new mission assignment in Kenya. My brother and sister went back to Africa with them, but I stayed in Texas to go to college. It was hard knowing that my parents were all the way across the ocean, but being so independent gave me a can-do spirit. I got to set up my own little apartment for the first time, and discovered hidden treasures in thrift stores and garage sales.

Since I was experienced in the art of using-what-you-have, I could make it homey, even though I was on a budget and my parents were far away. I eventually finished my degree and started my career as an office manager for an international software company. It helped having the support of my soon-to-be-husband all throughout my high-school and college years, and he's an international kid too! In fact, marrying him at age 21 was the best decision I've ever made. Born in Australia and raised in Papua, New Guinea, he was familiar with the lifestyle I grew up in as a missionary kid. After 9 years of marriage, we had 2 amazing daughters, who are now in college. We reside as empty nesters in Grapevine, Texas and have been married for 28 years.

Share with us what your business is and why you wanted to start this business.

When my kids started elementary school, I didn't want to go back to working for someone else. I wanted a flexible schedule, so that I could work around my family. For many years, my husband and I remodeled several of our own homes from top to bottom, and I decorated them. I had a knack for creating an inviting space that didn't feel pretentious and stuffy. I created unique spaces with antiques, thrift store finds, and repurposed furniture, giving it a collected, but not overly decorated feel. Friends started encouraging me to help them with their homes, and soon word got out. I quickly realized that this could be a lucrative business. It was something I was good at and passionate about.

This is when I began to think that maybe, this was my new calling. I started with my "walk through consultations" for the DIY client. I would spend two hours with the client, talking about anything in their home that they had questions about. I also began my "one day design," where I would take what the client already had and rework it in a new way. I created a website which became the portfolio of my work and got certified in Interior Design at a local community college. In 2002, DecRenew Interiors by Ruthie Staalsen was born. DecRenew Interiors is now a full-service design business. We handle design projects and remodels from the design implementation, all the way to the finite finishing touches.

What have you learned about yourself in running your business?

I have responded to adversity with a positive attitude. As a family growing up overseas, this philosophy was *crucial*, because our circumstances were not always the easiest. We had to train ourselves to find the good in all circumstances, regardless of whether they were comfortable ones. There was always something positive we could find, even in the worst situations. Once I started my business, I realized how much I truly sought people in my life that are of the same mindset.

Life is challenging, and running a business is no easy task. I've tried to respond to the obstacles and storms that have been placed in my life, and use them as tools to help me become a better human being. Some of the storms I've faced have crippled me with such pain and anguish, I often felt like I could hardly breathe. However, I do look back now and feel those struggles prepared me for each phase in my life, especially in my business. One of the hardest, and most rewarding things I had to learn was the importance of being *"joyful in hope, patient in affliction" and "faithful in prayer." (Romans 12:12) Sometimes* the hardest experiences in life are the most rewarding. It all depends on how you respond to the circumstances you have been given,

I've learned to disconnect from work. Learning to disconnect is just as important as working hard. Because I am a creative person, I often find that I have a hard time turning my mind off. It took me years to recognize when I need rest, especially now that technology is constantly at our fingertips. About 2 years into my business, my husband brought to my attention that I was becoming over-worked and over-stressed, and that I was letting my work stress affect others around me in a negative way. I was juggling so many hats as a mom and business owner, that I was working around the clock. I agreed that this was taking a toll on my family life and we decided we had to change something so I could unplug.

So, we bought an RV, and started camping on weekend getaways as a family. Right away, it became a home away from home for us and allowed us to totally relax. No phones, no chores, and no work to distract us. It re-opened my eyes to what really matters in life and brought my life back to the basics. For me, being out in nature forced me to appreciate the simplicity of life and remind me of my childhood. It has helped me to be a better mom, wife, and friend, and has created some incredible memories and traditions for our family.

I'm capable of more than I think I am. At times, I wonder how on earth I would learn all that had to be learned about running a design business. In the beginning, I had to do a lot of the groundwork for the business, including the stuff I wasn't so good at. I had to stretch my skills in many areas and learn things that I knew nothing about. We often think, "I could never do that," and then soon realize that we can do more than we think.

I can't do everything for my business alone. When I first started my business, I felt like I should know everything and do everything. Over time, I have learned that it is not possible for me to do everything for my business. I had to eventually hire people to help me. I have come to the realization that I do have some control issues and needed to let that go. Some things may not be done exactly how I would do it, but it gets done well, and that is more than fabulous. I have learned to trust the people I have hired, so that they can take the reins occasionally. After I did that a few times, it freed me to focus on all the things that I am good at, and allowed me to hire the experts to take care of the rest. One of the most important lessons I have learned as a business owner, is that it is okay to need help sometimes.

What three things do you wish you would have known when you started?

Each day brings surprises and many obstacles. There are ups and downs and many no's. If you are not the type of person that can go with the flow, that will be the first thing you will learn as an entrepreneur.

The part of your business that you will love is only about 20% of it. The other 80% is the grind work that every business owner must do: the bookkeeping, billing, phone calls, replying to emails, thank you cards, and taxes are just a few of those things. Even though this aspect to running your own business is tedious, it is well worth it when the result is in sight.

The entrepreneur life can be lonely. I had to force myself be a part of a community of entrepreneurs like myself. I grew up surrounded by community and so I know how important it is. At first, it was hard to connect with the right people. When I found a group of likeminded creatives at a design bloggers conference, it was an instant bonding experience and is now a place where I can share my struggles, hardships, and laugh out loud experiences. I have learned from some of the best designers in the industry. Some that are now lifetime friends, and they have stretched me and mentored me, into a better designer.

What 3 characteristics describe what has made you successful and why?

I believe we have all been given a purpose in life. Growing up, I was surrounded by people that owned the gifts and talents that God had given them. I watched parents, neighbors, and friends purposefully seek out these gifts, and use them to help others. Linguists, teachers, pilots, translators, anthropologists, doctors, nurses, mechanics, cooks, and photographers, are just a few of these gifts I encountered. Each one of them used their unique gifts they had been given to help others. I watched ordinary people being used for extraordinary things. Due to this, I have gained confidence in the gift of creativity that God has given me and it's up to me to use my gifts to honor Him.

I am truly blessed to be able to see beauty in small things. I have seen how my creativity can be used to enrich the lives of others, and that is what makes me get up each day with enthusiasm and excitement. Sometimes, we are surrounded by people that are so capable in their gifts that it can be discouraging; making us feel like we are not good enough. Do not disregard your gifts as things that cannot be used for good just because you do not have what someone else does. We are each uniquely different in what we can do; all of us vital to the bigger picture. Don't listen to that voice inside you that makes you doubt yourself and what God has given you. Use what you have, and know that sometimes, even the small things make the biggest impact. Doing what you are called to do is an honor and blessing not only to others, but to YOU. Being a designer has taught me that *"Life is never made unbearable by circumstances, but only by lack of meaning and purpose"* (*Victor E. Frankl*).

I refuse to let fear stop me from moving forward. It feels awful to fail, but I have learned that failure is not the end of the world, especially when you know that you have a purpose. Your purpose is what reminds you to keep trying. This means that every time you fail, you get stronger. Pride can be your biggest enemy, because no one wants to admit that they have failed. There were days where I cried ugly tears and wanted to quit right then and there. Sometimes it is so hard to keep going. However, pushing through my failure and applying what I learned through experience, is why my company is where it is today. The moment you feel like you want to quit, is the moment you need to keep going. If I had not had to fall on my face, I would not have learned some important lessons that have helped me run my business over the years.

I have learned how to be a good communicator and mediator. Being a good communicator is a huge part of owning a design business. I am in people's homes daily. That can be intimidating to clients, because their home is their personal and private space. So, it is very important that they feel comfortable with our relationship. To have that, I purposely listen well, ask lots of questions, and truly show interest in getting to know them. I strive to have a spirit of openness, so that I can be as authentic as possible. I have learned to read people well, and I believe that this skill stems from growing up in so many different cultures. I had to learn to become a good mediator when couples have difficulties deciding on major decisions for their home. This means listening to each of their preferences and softly guiding them to a solution that they both feel comfortable with. It is important to keep in mind that *"Your smile is your logo, your personality is your business card, how you leave others feeling after they have had an experience with you, becomes your trademark" (Zig Ziglar)*. If you read my reviews, you will see that this skill is mentioned often, and has become part of my brand.

How have you defined your voice in your market?

I started a blog so that I could share my decorating ideas with others. I shared projects I was working on, completed new ideas, current trends and DIY projects so that others could be inspired by the things I love. I continue to post helpful information to my readers to educate and inspire them with their own interior decorating. Many people tell me on their first appointment that they watched my social media and avidly read my blog for months before they decided to hire me. It gave them an idea of what I am all about and helped them build a trust bond, even before I meet them.

I wasn't afraid to showcase my work. When I first got started, I volunteered to speak at garden clubs, women's clubs, and leadership events to get my name out there. I showed up at trade shows where I gained some new clients, and started writing articles for blogs and local newspapers and magazines. Over the years, I have submitted my work to magazines, both locally and internationally, and have even been published in some big-name shelter magazines. It is so important to not be afraid of putting yourself out there. Had I not, I might not have been given some of these opportunities over the years.

I created a strong online presence. I hired a marketing company after about 5 years of trying to do it on my own, and that helped me tremendously. I am very active on social media and often find that it is the best way to represent your brand. I have made friends with other interior designers in my industry, and keep up with those relationships weekly. I am a member of several Facebook groups that spur me on, and teach me daily about my business and how to market myself better.

I donate my time to local Dallas charities and I am involved in my community. I am also a member of the Interior Design Society. This has helped me connect with local design organizations so that I can network and collaborate with the best in my industry. You will find that it is so rewarding to donate time to others. Seeing how a community functions can often give you new perspectives, and allows you to connect to others in a way that you cannot experience from behind a computer screen.

What would you advise someone who is struggling with building their brand?

Ideally, it is best if you can start your business with amazing branding; having all your ducks lined neatly in a row. For me, it did not exactly work that way. From the start, I was organized and always made it a priority to have an agenda. However, it has taken years for me to slowly build my brand. At first, I just stepped out and did what I felt was right. I started with some of the things that I really felt I was good at, and then allowed those things lead to other things. Over time, it became clearer to me what my brand should be all about.

Do not feel like you must have everything perfectly in order before you start your business. Just start somewhere, and you will slowly find yourself moving forward and making progress. Over thinking things can paralyze you. It is great to be a person that researches and considers things before jumping off the cliff. However, do not let that stop you from taking a risk occasionally, and adding your own twist and perspective to a project. Originality will help you with moving forward to greater things.

What are you about? What is your story, background, why do you do what you do?

My main objective is to create environments that are gathering places for families and friends to do life together. However, I am about more than that. I believe that the home is a special hub for the best moments in life. It's the place where you watch your kids dance around the kitchen. It is where you and your hubby carry your kids to the bed because they fell asleep on the couch. It's where your daughter brings a boy home for the first time, and where your family laughs around the dinner table so hard that you choke on your food. Home is where real life happens, and sometimes real life is a little bit messy. That is why I want the homes I decorate to be a place for peace and solitude. Our society is so busy and hurried that spending time at home is almost a lost art.

My goal is to connect these wonderful moments of life to the home through interior design. I have a different perspective on design in that it isn't totally about a specific look. It's more about finding the soul of the people living in the home, and helping the client find what makes them feel good to be surrounded by. Decorating is about creating a quality of life, a beauty that nourishes the soul. Our homes should reflect what we are about, our beliefs, our experiences and family traditions. Because after all, homes are not just about nice things, they're about a place where you want to spend time. **I want to be known as the designer that connects these dots.**

Budget- friendly design is what my business was founded on. I want the average person to feel like they too can have a beautiful home that they love. I offer a 2 hour walk through consultation for the DIY'er, where I give them ideas and inspiration to spur them on. Or I can take the entire project on and make it happen for them from start to finish. I feel the happiest in my career when I meet with a client and as I'm leaving, they are pulling out of their driveway at the same time, headed to the paint store so they can start painting with the colors I suggested.

From the start, I always wanted my business to be able to support other missionaries. That dream has come true, and we support about 5 families doing different mission work all over the world. It is so rewarding to be able to give back to missions after so many families and individuals supported my family growing up.

Staying motivated when things don't seem to be coming together is a challenge at times. How do you motivate yourself? What would you advise someone else?

Choose your tribe carefully. I have found people who challenge and stretch me to be the best I can be. "Be around the light bringers, the magic makers, the world shifters, the game shakers. They challenge you, break you open, uplift and expand you. They don't let you play small with your life. These heartbeats are your people. These people are your tribe" (Author Unknown).

Create small things to look forward to. Set small attainable goals that create a sense of achievement. Reward yourself for finishing tasks and getting through things that are not as fun. It spurs you on to keep going and gives you a sense of accomplishment.

Push through the mundane days because there are a lot of them; full of hardship and frustration. Sometimes we don't "feel" like doing things, but you have got to learn to push through them anyway. Growing a business takes years of perseverance to succeed, and certainly doesn't happen overnight. You don't get what you WISH FOR, you get what you WORK FOR. People often say to me "you are so lucky that you have been so successful", it has nothing to do with luck, it has to do with a ton of extremely hard work that has paid off!

What has been your most effective marketing tool/strategy and why?

Referrals, Referrals, Referrals. Do your best work for your clients so that they are happy. This will make them talk about you, and share their experience with others. However, as you know, it isn't always possible to please everyone. I do everything in my power to make the client feel satisfied with the job I have done. I will bend over backwards to make sure I leave the job with as much enthusiasm and excitement that I had when I started the job. Referrals are your biggest marketing tool.

Teach others what you know – I found that a great way to get your name out there is to be open about sharing your ideas and inspiration with others. Everyone is out there to learn. Sharing the valuable information, you have, is an effective way to gain respect from your followers. On social media, I follow people that are willing to give me nuggets of inspiration. This helps me learn new things, and allows me to take my business to the next level. I try to do the same thing so people can learn from me as well.

Take advantage of websites and social media. I joined several online websites where decorators can create their own design portfolio. I created galleries of my own work, and started getting a name for myself by answering questions and giving advice when asked. I also have a strong Facebook page and I am very involved with Instagram. I try to post photos daily that inspire me, in hopes that they will inspire others as well. Instagram stories has also become a great way for me to share "behind the scenes" of a typical day of decorating an entire home. This includes shopping for accessories, and even photo shoots. Any way that I can give people a glimpse into what they may experience if they hire me, is a plus. Your online presence makes your Google analytics stronger and is a powerful way for search engines to find your website.

One of the biggest struggles women entrepreneurs have is how to price themselves. What advice would you share about pricing your services and offerings?

When you get started, you may not be able to charge the typical going rate, because you are trying to gain credibility. Look at your market and see what your typical client would be happy to pay. However, don't underprice yourself. You are valuable, and you need to make it worth your while. At first, you might have to start by volunteering and doing things you don't love doing as much, just to get your business started. I remember swapping services or doing a few things for free at the beginning. However, you must make sure you set boundaries, otherwise you will get taken for granted. As you gain experience, you will be able to be more selective with what jobs you take and how much you charge. Every 2-3 years I have evaluated my pricing, and changed it accordingly. There have been times when I have cut my prices a bit when the economy has been lean. However, I always make sure I am making a decent profit. It is not a hobby, it is my livelihood.

What advice would you give to a woman entrepreneur who is ready to take her business to the next level?

Be bold and confident, it is contagious! Clients like to see that you carry yourself with confidence. If you would like to achieve success, it is important that you believe you are worthy. Your attitude and the way you present yourself is crucial to your success. Dress the part, it helps you hold your head high and gives you added confidence. It helps me communicate to others that I am knowledgeable and competent. Carry yourself with boldness, but remember that humility is even more important. Nothing is more obnoxious than an arrogant person who acts superior to others. Humility is the most attractive attribute.

Find others that you respect and admire in your industry. Surround yourself with experienced professionals that have gone before you. Purposely surround yourself with them, so that you can ask questions about their successes and failures. Sign up for workshops and classes. Listen to podcasts, and be a part of Facebook groups where information is shared and questions are asked that you can learn from. There is so much value in learning from others mistakes and successes; things that are even more valuable than information you can get in a classroom setting. Experience speaks volumes.

Don't just be comfortable where you are. Take on challenges that make you grow. The task may seem daunting but try the things you are afraid of doing. Volunteer for the things you have longed to do, but felt scared to. You won't grow if you don't try new things. You own your life, so make it happen. I've found that if it feels scary at first, it is probably worth doing.

You are going to get criticism. You can't please everyone all the time. You must learn to let this roll off your shoulders. It can cripple you, if you take everything everyone says to you to heart. Sometimes you just must let things go. There have been times where people have discouraged me, and told me things I had ideas about weren't possible. Those were the times I've had to change my mindset and continue forward with an even greater determination. You must always remember that you know yourself and what you are capable of better than anyone else. No one can tell you what you can and can't do.

What "must have" resources would you recommend someone use in their business?

An organized office space. That doesn't mean it should be the best of the best. My first office was in a closet in our guest room. It was tiny, but we turned it into a place that was functional and very well organized. Having a place to focus and get away from the noise of life, can make a huge impact on your productivity.

Don't be afraid to ask for reviews. Reviews are crucial in this online world we live in. They can encourage you, and give future clients insight as to how you work with others and what you stand for. My reviews are what get me about 50% of my business. They have helped me build my brand into what it is today, I'm about people and relationships while creating beautiful homes.

A website with professional photography. If you can't afford an experienced photographer, find a student that is talented that can take good photos of your work. This can be a way to give someone else an opportunity to gain experience and put their work out there. Be sure that the photos you put out there represent your work, and who you are. As a designer, photos are often the first thing people see about you when they are thinking of hiring you. Therefore, it is so important to have photos that are true to your work. You do not have to have a professional photographer to do that.

Hire good people that represent you well. For me, I am diligent about creating personal relationships with my contractors, workrooms, and painters. This helps your business to function as a well-oiled machine, instead of several separate parts. Don't rush this process. Truly seek out a team with good values, hard work ethic and a can-do attitude. They are an extension of your brand.

Pick a social media platform that works for you and go with it. It seems like every time I turn around, there is a new social media app to be a part of. This can be overwhelming. I've chosen a few that work for me and have stuck with those. Instagram is one of them, because I can post photos of my work, as well as ideas that inspire my followers. Be good at one or two of them, and don't try to spread yourself too thin. If you aren't good at this kind of thing, then hire someone to help you even if it is an intern! It is not always something that comes naturally to everyone. Regardless, it is crucial that you have an online presence.

What makes you a woman that is making an impact?

I have learned to run in my own lane. I made a purposeful change and decided that I was going to march to my own drum. In this social media world, I was constantly comparing myself to others. While that was very motivating at times, it really began to cripple me. Remember that "comparison is the thief of joy." I would start second guessing what I was doing, and began to feel self-doubt creeping its way into my confidence. I constantly must remind myself to rest in the promise that God has given me, and accept that He has different plans for all of us. We can't compare our Chapter 1 to someone else's Chapter 40. Define success on your own terms, achieve it by your own rules so you build a life YOU are proud of. Write your own story, that is what we were created to do.

I try to lead with integrity. Everyone that is on my team is treated the same. Whether you are my assistant or the guy installing the wood floors. I strive to reinforce to them that they are needed and valued because they are NEEDED. I've learned that when I honor and respect the people that work with me, they honor and respect me. Treating others with respect enables you to have good relationships with the people you hire, and makes them work harder. Be teachable it is a good characteristic to have and makes you approachable.

I want to be the person others want to be with. I consciously try to walk in the room and be the one that brings joy. Not a fake joy, but a true joy that makes people look forward to seeing me. When you encourage and uplift others, the mood and vibe instantly changes and you create a positive work environment for everyone. This same concept is carried into my home as well. As the mom, I'm conscious about the mood I create for the day in our home. I'm far from perfect but really try.

I don't do things half way. I go the extra mile for people. I don't start something and then not finish it. If I commit to something, I do it. I am extremely loyal, and have found that to be one of my best assets. My design business is not just about making homes beautiful, it's about making a change for the better in the lives of those I encounter each day.

I'm an overcomer. In elementary school, I was diagnosed with dyslexia. Dyslexia made school incredibly hard for me, and I had to work twice as hard as my classmates to succeed. I also struggled with eye issues and wore very thick glasses that didn't help with my self-esteem. My parents enrolled me in a dyslexic school that taught me new ways to learn. I was taught not to become a victim of dyslexia, and instead, learned how to be an overcomer and an extremely hard worker. The school, along with my parents, gave me the "don't give up" attitude that helped me gain the strong belief I have in myself today. We are all given weaknesses, but we have a heavenly father that will provide strength in those weaknesses. Where we are weak, He is strong. I saw God provide strength for me growing up, and I am thankful that He fills up what is lacking in me.

I celebrate others successes and achievements. I choose to be just as enthusiastic about the success of others as I am about my own. Not everyone will celebrate with you in your joys and triumphs. Don't resent others success. Instead, choose to be bigger than that! Be the one that is full of positive things to say, not the one that is always thinking of the negatives. You gain so much as a person from celebrating life with other people. It helps you to remember that not everything in life is about you.

I like to have FUN. I often ask people what they do for fun. So many times, they don't know how to answer that question, because they don't know how to play. Life can't always be serious. Working hard and playing hard go hand in hand. Life is so much richer when you do things that are crazy, fun, and unexpected. Do things out of the ordinary. It is exhilarating and good for the soul. I have found that having fun with the simple things is contagious, others want to join in. Have a bit of fun every day, get your team involved, it's good for your health.

Wild card question! Share whatever you would like the women reading your story to know about you, your business, or your journey.

Set guidelines for your business. One of my priorities in starting my own business, was that my family came first. Especially when my girls were young. If things with work began to interfere with investing time with my family, I learned to lighten my load. There were some amazing opportunities that came my way, and I had to pass them up even when they could have launched my business forward. My husband and I stuck to our priorities, and that made it easier to say no. You get to define success in your own terms and set your own rules for different seasons in your life. Now, years later, my girls are in college and I'm able to take on more and accept projects that are more time consuming. Set the guidelines and know you are making those choices because you have priorities. Don't rob yourself of the joy that being an entrepreneur allows you. You get to call the shots and prioritize your business for YOUR life.

It takes years to build a business. It has taken endurance, drive, motivation, persistence, passion, and commitment; the list goes on and on. These qualities are so important, because without them, you would quit. You will put time and money into doing certain things and then nothing comes of it, at least not right away. Growing your business will be frustrating and test your patience at times. It won't happen overnight, but all the effort you put into it is not wasted. Things will happen eventually. Each obstacle leads you to the next thing. My obstacles were stepping stones to my next successes. Don't give up too soon, press on.

Schedule time on your calendar for YOU. I use to feel like taking time for myself wasn't important. I have discovered that it is crucial. I now schedule time on my calendar for me time and consider it an appointment that can't be broken. Thanks to my dad for that advice! I have had times where I was so stressed, I could hardly think straight. Stress makes you believe that everything must be done right away. I've learned that it doesn't. Each day I get better about prioritizing myself.

Don't be afraid to be authentic about your struggles. Your failures can prevent others from making the same mistakes. Let others learn from you. Don't pretend like everything is easy. Sometimes the best thing you can be is vulnerable: about your failures and hardships, successes and triumphs. Being in business for yourself has amazing benefits but it is far from easy.

I created a policy that I don't work for family and friends. My relationships are important to me, and mixing work with my personal life is a place where I decided to draw the line. In the business of design, this policy is so important. It is easy for things to become complicated when you are mixing friends and family with your work life. I learned that for me personally, it was important to keep the two separate.

Set business hours – I have hours of business that I make sure my clients are aware of. You must set these guidelines for yourself, especially today where we have our phones with us 24/7. Sometimes this can make clients think that you are obligated to respond as soon as they text or call, even if it is after hours. Of course, my clients are my priority and if they leave me a message after business hours because it is a true emergency, I am going to respond. However, I had to set guidelines so I can turn off my work and have a personal life.

Learn more about Ruthie Staalsen

Ruthie Staalsen of DecRenew Interiors is an internationally renowned Interior Designer in the Dallas area with over 15 years of experience. She was a nominee for the 2016 New Trad Home Rising Stars of Design from Traditional Home. She has been voted one of the "Top 15 Decorators in Dallas," awarded "Tops in Tarrant, Best in Industry" by Society Life Magazine, "Rave Reviews" by Houzz, as well as "Best of Houzz" for Service and Design since 2012. Her work has been featured in publications such as "Traditional Home Magazine" Great Kitchens, and "Elite Monde", a Lifestyle and Fashion Magazine in Dubai. Ruthie's mission is to connect life and home through design. Her passion is merging the souls of people, places and experiences so memories can begin and traditions can continue.

Website: www.ruthiestaalsen.com

ANGIE LEIGH MONROE

Founder of D.I.V.A.S Impact

Tell us a little about yourself. We want to learn about the person behind the brand.

If you have ever heard me speak, or listened to my radio shows you will know I have a bit of a Texas twang. In high school, it was much worse, and I was in drama. One day I excitedly ran into my drama classroom calling out my drama instructors name. "Mr. B., Mr. B." before I could get anything else out this tall man of perfect poise and stature turned facing me and with the sternest booming voice I had ever heard him use, said; "Young lady, as long as you sound like a hick you will never amount to anything." Have you ever had the air knocked out of you, that is exactly what happened to me? The next day I transferred out of drama and did not step back on the stage for 25 years.

I would like to say that was a one-time occurrence, but because I aligned my beliefs about myself with the words from my drama instructor, I had what they called a series of continuing violations. I was always good enough to do what people wanted me to do, but I was never given what I truly sought after in the workforce. I accelerated rapidly while serving in the military, or working in the for profit and nonprofit world, but it was still not where I KNEW I should be. Then it happened, I looked myself in the mirror one day and said enough is enough, I will no longer believe that who I am is not enough! That was the day I removed the mask and began moving thru life asking for and getting what I was wanted from life and all it had to offer.

Share with us what your business is and why you wanted to start this business.

I was standing on the stage at a friend's conference, as the Emcee. Although my role up to that moment had been me, being goofy and keeping the energy up in the room, the atmosphere now was being shifted. I had been asked to share a personal story as a testimony for a non-profit I was connected with.

The electric buzz of fun energy in the air, I simply said to the ladies, "Can I be authentic with you for a minute?" immediately the room fell silent, including the air system. I could feel trembling in my legs, my mouth was as dry as the Sahara, and all I wanted to do was cut tail and run. But this had been my secret desire, and it had just been handed to me. I stood up there, and shared my story, and as I walked off that stage that day (almost 25 years to the day since I quit drama) I felt like I had stepped into my skin!

Immediately I was brought to tears to think about how many women GIVE UP on their dreams. It might have been a life altering moment that had them settling for less than they were created for. It might have been a gradual giving up of themselves for their husbands, and children. Whatever it was, I knew that if I could step back on the stage after 25 years, then I could help others achieve their dreams as well!

What have you learned about yourself in running your business?

The biggest thing I have learned is that I have not been a very good friend to women. Yep, I said it! I was more comfortable working and being friends with men. Although I work with men and women, I am reminded on a continual basis how cruel we women can be to each other. So many times, I am sitting across from a lady who has been held back in life by an action from another woman. Maybe it was a female boss who had it out for her, a friend that slept with her husband, or a colleague who used her as a stepping stone to a promotion. I would like to say I have being a great friend down to a perfect science now, but that simply is not true. Every day I am working to make sure my clients/friends get the very best from me. This does not mean that they always get what they want from me, but I do strive to give them what they need from me.

What three things do you wish you would have known when you started?

- How distracting the little things can be
- When to say NO
- How to automate my business for efficiency

What 3 characteristics describe what has made you successful and why?

- Strategic
- Funny
- Relational

How have you defined your voice in your market?

I help people ALIGN themselves with strategic relationships to move them along as they ACTIVATE their dreams, and teach them ways to make slight adjustments to CALIBRATE the life of their dreams.

Angie Leigh Monroe, Inc. is my corporation, I speak, write, coach, and train under that name. We will be launching the Angie Leigh Monroe Radio show in February. I am also the founder of D.I.V.A.S. Impact where we help women overcome obstacles, find clarity and encounter even more opportunities. We have an online magazine, our Daily DIVAS blog which is launching February 1st. We launched our D.I.V.A.S. Impact Radio show on January 2nd, 2017.Our Facebook page alone has over 38K followers.

What would you advise someone who is struggling with building their brand?

Be True to You: First, identify who you are, not who everyone else says you are but what influential thing do you dream about doing or being? Then identify the things that you make up that dream. There are tons of tiny things that make up being a speaker, boutique owner, or nonprofit leader. When you identify what, those components are where you can drill down to your target niche and the area of expertise you bring to the table. When you operate in your expertise, and who you authentically are, then you free yourself from trying to be something you are not and can naturally and confidently promote yourself and what you do.

Staying motivated when things don't seem to be coming together is a challenge at times. How do you motivate yourself? What would you advise someone else?

I am challenge driven, so I set benchmarks for me. Most of the time when things aren't coming together for me it is because I have not put enough stepping stones in place on my way to reach a goal. Creighton Abrams said: "When eating an elephant, take one bite at a time." So, break things down in manageable pieces because I know that if I string enough small successes together they will lead to BIG successes.

Here is a sample of the process I use and it works for anything:

- ✓ Goal: Take shower & wash hair
- ✓ Things needed: Shower, soap, loofah water, shampoo, conditioner, 2 towels, clean clothes, blow drier, round brush, hair products
- ✓ Things to do: Turn on water, adjust water to right temperature, get towels from linen closet, clean clothes from closet & dresser, wet loofah, add soap to loofah, wash body with loofah, rinse body until it is rid of soap, wet hair, apply shampoo to head and massage into hair, rinse, repeat, add conditioner to head and massage into hair, rinse until water runs clear, wring out hair, use 1 towel and twist around hair on top of head, use 2nd towel to dry body off, get dressed, apply hair products to hair, blow dry hair, style hair with round brush, hang towels up to dry. YOUR DONE

What has been your most effective marketing tool / strategy and why?

Majority of our marketing is on social media. It has been a great avenue to reach out to potential clients, engage with them, and build trust. Building trust is important to me, I want to trust the people who are leading me, so I want to be sure we are trustworthy for the people we are leading. Social media affords us the opportunity hear what our audience is asking for, and develop content that will meet them where they are at. I also do a lot of networking at live events to meet people face to face.

One of the biggest struggles women entrepreneurs have is how to price themselves. What advice would you share about pricing your services and offerings?

Research, Research, and Research. Today, it is so simple to find out what the fair market value is for your services. Then you must believe that you are worth what the fair market value says you are, and you must deliver on that belief!

Your fair market value is what you market on your website, and in marketing materials. However, we know there are always those clients you would love to work with, they may be a dream clients, or a passion project. You have the ability as an entrepreneur to adjust your fee. My challenge to you is to have that fee already set. Even with your dream client or passion project you are still going to have the same amount of work. Too many times I see clients cut their prices in half, and then they are stressing as they struggle to deliver something that is not paying enough.

What advice would you give to a woman entrepreneur who is ready to take her business to the next level?

Find someone who has achieved some of the things you want to achieve, learn from them what worked, and what didn't. Ask them about expenses they incurred, laws and regulations that you might have to submit to. Ask them to mentor you, but also be willing to pay them for their time. Their wisdom in the areas you are moving into will save you countless hours and many, many dollars!

What "must have" resources would you recommend someone use in their business?

- ✓ Asana to manage our projects, (Your to do list is a project)
- ✓ Zendesk for management of emails coming in
- ✓ Canva & PicMonkey for shareable social media graphics
- ✓ Misaic's Extreme Marketing Machine: landing pages, tracking codes, and email capture

What makes you a woman that is making an impact?

- ✓ I walk in my Destiny (purpose)
- ✓ I have been Inspired, and I inspire others
- ✓ I have found Victory, and help others be Victorious
- ✓ I am Accountable to others and I hold others Accountable
- ✓ I live to be a Sister to many!
- ✓ That is what makes me a D.I.V.A.S. Diva and I make my impact by equipping and empowering other women to do the same.

Wild card question! Share whatever you would like the women reading your story to know about you, your business, or your journey.

I understand shame, and not forgiving yourself for past mistakes. I lived that life for a very long time. If you or someone you know is caught up in a thick fog of shame, let me help. I do not want to publicly blast anyone, but I will reach out my hand and help you navigate the way to walk out of the darkness. Because you flourish in the light!

Learn more about Angie Leigh Monroe

Angie Leigh Monroe, a native Texan and Navy veteran, is the D.I.V.A.S. Diva. She founded D.I.V.A.S. Impact - a global movement set up to change the way women think and speak about themselves and others. She helps people identify and obliterate obstacles that hold them back from finding their purpose. Her ability to ALIGN you with strategic partnerships, ACTIVATE your purpose and CALIBRATE your potential to live life to its fullest is what makes her the consummate DIVA. Angie lives in Euless, TX and loves time with her husband, children and grandchildren.

Website: AngieLeighMonroe.com

NIKKY PHINYAWATANA
Creator and Owner of Dallas' highly acclaimed, award-winning Asian Mint Restaurant

Tell us a little about yourself. We want to learn about the person behind the brand.

I am first and foremost a mom to a 7-year-old son and a 3-year-old daughter, a wife to my loving husband of 12 years, owner and founder of the Asian Mint restaurant group. I am a born idealistic entrepreneur. I get very excited about taking an idea and turning it into reality. I love supporting my community and people who want to follow their passion.

Share with us what your business is and why you wanted to start this business.

I am the owner of two, soon to be three award-winning Asian fusion restaurants in Dallas, Texas branded as Asian Mint. I wanted to open a restaurant because I saw a disconnect in marketplace between people asking for more Asian cuisine and having knowledge about it.

I saw the opportunity to educate and engage with guest by making the environment more approachable. I observed people leaving various types of Asian restaurants complaining about their clothes smelling like fried food or feeling over "soy-ed" with sodium. They were saying they didn't feel like the meals were fresh products. I saw this as an opportunity to bring Asian food into a better light, so for me, a light bulb went on.

When I was designing the restaurant, I wanted to make sure it would always feel and smell clean. I also wanted to provide fresh and healthy cuisine that tastes amazing. My desire was to represent multiple Asian cultures. Our menu comprises of Thai dishes, Japanese dishes, Chinese dishes and Sushi. We have simple preparation in a nice modern clean and chic atmosphere.

Our guests enjoy the modern atmosphere. In the case of most Asian restaurants, getting a nice glass of wine or cocktail during your meal is not the norm, nor is experiencing a very good cappuccino and dessert at the end of your meal. At Asian Mint, we have it all. Our guests can enjoy a nice drink, coffee, and dessert while continuing their lunch or dinner conversations. We explore opportunities in the marketplace to fill a need that is not currently being served and created our own innovative fusion.

Something that greatly influences my work is my life which is interwoven with multi-culturalism. I see things differently being raised in two cultures, both the United States, specifically in Texas, and in Thailand. By having a dual cultural background, I see things from different perspectives, which greatly influences what I bring to the restaurant.

My background shaped my creation of fusion aspects, not only in the food, but also in the cultural atmosphere and service in the restaurant. My multicultural background has helped me put that all together in a unique and fresh way that feels very authentic to who I am. I believe this creates a broader multicultural appeal to a lot of different people. They desire to be adventurous by exploring and experiencing something different while, at the same time, have the familiarity of being home. It's both authentic AND new.

What have you learned about yourself and running your own business?

I started my first restaurant at age 27. In my mind, I had nothing to lose. I had recently gotten married and I wanted to do something that mattered with the few dollars we had, so we just went for it. I jumped into the deep end head first, never owning a restaurant. My experience consisted of being a server and delivering food which had me running in and out of restaurants and kitchens. Seeing the ins and outs of the restaurant business from that point of view, I knew immediately that I wanted to do my own thing. I wanted to create a new experience, something that was lacking in the industry. I also knew that I would have to learn how to manage people and delegate projects. I have learned through the years how important teamwork is to the success of any business and thank goodness, I had my husband on my team.

I realized I would need more of a support team to make the operational side more successful if we were going to grow our business. During the first 10 years, we did it literally without a manual. Nothing was written down, not even our recipes. I realized that every time we trained someone new we had to keep repeating ourselves and lacked a consistent central resource. We knew there had to be an easier way to deliver consistent training and maintain skilled staff levels.

I've learned that documenting "processes" can be extremely beneficial. We now implement structured processes as part of our training. We also spend time familiarizing new hires with the culture of our restaurants. Through developing the training I have learned how to manage and coach in order to get the best out of people. This has been a win-win for everyone. It's probably the most valuable lesson I have personally gained from as well!

What 3 things do you wish you would have known when you started?

Initially, I would say that I don't think I would have changed anything because that's how I learned my lessons. Maybe if I had

had the documentation I mentioned above, I might have been able to grow faster. But, then, at the same time, I started a family and doing other things in order to establish a more balanced life. With everything in place, things might have slowed me down more or it might have sped me up. You really don't know. I am glad I learned the lessons I did. It's made me a stronger person.

If asked for three things, I would say: 1. **pre-plan** and create specific goals, 2. **determine what processes, people and systems** need to be in place before you launch, and 3. **hire a team and delegate**. Executing this plan gives you a better chance of reaching your desired goals.

Describe three characteristics that have made you successful and why?

I am a confident risk taker, have a strong and determined work ethic to make sure I succeed, and have humble gratitude. To be a confident risk taker, I had to trust my gut and believe in myself because if you don't believe in yourself, you can't really accomplish anything. Also, you cannot be afraid of failing. If you learn from your mistakes you'll move closer to your succeed.

I am also very action oriented with strong determination. There are a lot of individuals out there who don't want to put in the work they need to be successful. This is THE one thing that sets the successful people apart from the rest... they put in the hard work no matter the situation. That's where I'm different from most. I believe it takes dedication and hard work to make things happen and see your dreams take flight.

I have also learned to delegate, which is not something I always did, but when I learned how to let go and delegate, things started to shift for the better. Delegating has made all the difference. This has allowed me the time to concentrate and focus on being creative and coming up with fun ideas, all while allowing others to do what they are good at such as operations and finance.

I also hold onto a strong sense of humble gratitude for everything in my life. It guides everything I do. Without it, I don't think we would have the support team behind us to help us reach our goals. This also allows for more ideas to flow and creates for a great environment to connect with our guests. I listen to my community and I'm grateful for them. I believe this causes them to be more open about telling me what I'm doing right and wrong because they know that I will act. There's a trust that we have created due to this collective understanding.

How have you defined your voice in your market?

At the beginning, I researched and analyzed what other businesses were missing and paired that with my authentic self and intuition to form our voice. We are always about providing fresh Asian food at a great value. However, I have noticed that our voice evolves as we and our guests evolve. I have been fortunate enough to see changes with our guests and made a conscious decision to change with them. There's a lot of open communication with our guests, so new ideas and interactions are always unfolding. Currently, we are big on educating and inspiring the community. Not many restaurants are about educating and inspiring. We keep it fresh and innovative in our cuisine an in our voice.

What would you advise someone who is struggling in their brand?

I would advise them to get a brand specialist, a business coach, and/or join a mastermind team. It really helps to talk things out with someone who really knows how to put a plan together. If it's not your expertise or if it's not coming out the way you want, ask for help. Find specialists and learn from their experience. Engage those with the expertise.

How do you motivate yourself and what would you advise someone else?

My number one piece of advice is to keep moving forward no matter what. There are times when the going gets difficult, but I believe that every challenge can become a teachable opportunity. This is how I've grown and moved forward. No matter what, keep moving and ask: What can I learn from this? Why is this happening? What do I need to learn about this? What do I need to do and not do from this? How do I move forward? Is it a sign? Is it a lesson? Then, I listen for the message without an emotional attachment to it. This process takes practice, it doesn't come easy and I still get stuck more often than you can imagine. I often will stop when I'm stuck, and go get rejuvenated by visiting with my guests. I reconnect with why I do what I do, and that helps to motivate me again and again.

What has been your most effective marketing strategy and why?

The beauty of being a small business is flexibility and being able to communicate directly with your guests. Ask for feedback and they will tell you what they really want. My most effective marketing strategy is listening to my guests and delivering on their suggestions. I like keeping them informed and educating them on changes. Make sure your message is aligned with your mission and vision. Be clear internally and externally. Constantly be top of mind. We have reward programs; email newsletters, and social media posts that keep everyone thinking of Asian Mint as their favorite Asian restaurant.

What advice would you share about pricing yourself?

Plain and simple…Explore the market and explore your competitors and see what kind of clientele they are attracting. Then, price your prices based on the value you provide based on the clientele you want to attract.

What advice would you give to an entrepreneur who wants to take her business to the next level?

Make sure you have your team in place and that you can explain your mission, vision and your goals to make sure that they are aligned with what you desire to create. Hire professionals like an accountant, an attorney, a financial advisor and marketing professionals. Also, make sure you have a mastermind partner(s) to talk through ideas and challenges. Again, delegation is THE key. The more that you can take off of your plate the more you can focus on big picture strategy which will take you to the next level.

What must have resources would you recommend that people should have in their business?

All the above!

What makes you a woman who is making an impact?

I am making an impact because I see what a difference we make in terms of how our guests come in and how they leave. The difference is how we uplift their souls. At Asian Mint, we've had amazing moments and made long term relationships. I feel like when we're able to feed the soul, not just their stomach, they're able to go out and change the world. Just by doing that, I feel like I'm being impactful in our community and the world.

I am also making an impact through the social outreach that we do. I believe having a successful business allows you to give from your overflow and support the causes that are important to you. By doing so, we give back to the communities we serve such as supporting teachers and schools in our area. We help feed people in need. We also help to educate our communities about food, health, and following their passion. We have a passion for coaching and mentoring our staff regarding leadership and following their passions. One idea I have is to develop programs to help young women become entrepreneurs. I love being able to impact the lives of the young people who work with us. We want to help them grow personally and professionally. We see how amazing they are. I love helping them figure out what their passions are as well as how we can help develop their skills to either grow with us or become amazing in their own big way. My big mission is to inspire passion!

Wild card question! Share whatever you would like the women reading your story to know about you, your business, or your journey.

My big lessons…*don't compare someone else's end or middle to your beginning*…this is not a competition and there is more than enough. *Being able to give more than trying to get* is so much more fulfilling to me. Also, *be OK with "failures"*. I have had plenty of failures, but I'm okay with them. I would also say *PLAY BIG because it's more fun that way*. It is more challenging and scarier, but so much better! It takes the same amount of energy to do small as it is to do something big, so why not go big? Also, *learn something new every day and implement those lessons. Don't over schedule and leave time for new things and new opportunities to come in.* Also, *always be willing to help other human beings out.* Take people with you as you can't do it alone.

For Asian Mint, I see us being more impactful than just in Texas. I envision us someday being on the stock market with over 100 international locations so that we can share the love globally. It really is fun when I visualize that and ask how can we impact the world in a very positive way through the medium of Asian food and the culture of lifestyle we are creating. We have a very people-conscious way of running a business as it's not about the money…it's about the people and cultivating their passion.

For our next steps, I see us expanding our corporate team so that we can continue to grow and at the same time maintain the same level of outstanding quality and excellent guest satisfaction.

In closing, wherever you are going and whatever you are doing, believe in yourself. Put infrastructure into place at the beginning. Don't wait for growth to do it because that's when it gets crazy. Trust that it is going to happen. Create a plan and execute your plan! Follow your passion and don't let others talk you out of following your dreams.

Learn more about Nikky Phinyawatana

 Nikky Phinyawatana is a visionary entrepreneur--the creator and owner of Dallas' highly acclaimed, award-winning Asian Mint Restaurant. Recently, Asian Mint was awarded Dallas Eater's #1 Best Thai Food and Culture Map's Top 100 Restaurants. Asian Mint has received accolades from USA Today, Zagat, Dallas Observer, and D Magazine. Nikky infuses love and passion into her innovative Asian Fusion menus and into her dedication to the community--to giving back. She is a member of Les Dames d'Escoffier International-- which provides mentorship and scholarships for the next wave of women culinary students--as well as an active board member of the Greater Dallas Restaurant Association and board of trustee member of Texas Restaurant Association Education Foundation.

Website: www.asianmint.com

PEARL CHIARENZA
Owner of Bodyworks Health & Wellness Center

Tell us a little about yourself. We want to learn about the person behind the brand.

Originally, I'm from all over the United States. My dad was a Marine Corp veteran that sent him around the states and he served more than two and a half tours in Vietnam. I was born in California in 1964 and moved as an infant to North Carolina with my parents. While my dad served in Vietnam, my mom raised us in upstate New York until the third grade where we settled until my sophomore year of high school in Jacksonville, NC. Then, my parents moved our family to Florida We than had one last move to California after I graduated high school in 1982. I did not enjoy California and within the first year I decided I wanted to move back to Florida, but God had different plans for me!

All packed and ready to head back to Florida, I met the love of my life. I met Chuck at a company picnic at Knott's Berry Farm. As the saying goes, the rest is history. I moved in with Chuck and within two years we were married and started our family. At first, we lived in Virginia and then finally, we raised our two wonderful boys Matt (19) and Nate (17) in Florida.

My company is called Bodyworks Health & Wellness Center and I started my business after personally losing 57 pounds with our program. Before that I was a mortgage loan originator. With our move to Florida I found that the mortgage business was going to be much harder than expected. That was mostly due to the economy. My children were not happy with our neighborhood as we went from over ten boys in our neighborhood to three including my two, and after having a hysterectomy in my late 30's I started to struggle with weight.

I found our protein based weight loss program and after the success I had, I wanted to bring it to the community. I took a risk and left the mortgage world to venture into working on my own. I opened my first location in Lakeland, Florida in April 2011 and I opened my second location in Brandon, Florida in September 2011. I have the honor of coaching my clients to a healthier way of living by using our protein products, eating vegetables, salad and a healthy dinner.

What have you learned about yourself in running your business?

Over the years of being a business owner I have learned to stick to the integrity of treating others the way I would like to be treated and to rely on my coach to guide me through decisions or challenges I may have. I reach out to others to learn from their experiences and become quite involved in our community by giving back. Through my business, I sponsor a woman that has struggled from domestic violence gifting her with our program for three months. With my community involvement, I have become very resourceful. It is not uncommon for me to receive calls from others that are referred to me because they hear I may know someone that can help them. I am proud of the fact that no matter what, with God's guidance, I will be on the path He has for me with my business and life goals.

What three things do you wish you would have known when you started?

First, I wish I would have known that while I have a large heart for giving not everyone I partner with will have the same goal. So, aligning with likeminded people is important.

Second, when I look back I wish I had hired a web designer at the start of my business. Lastly, finding the right branding expert earlier in my business would have enabled to get my message out clearly at the start of my business.

What 3 characteristics describe what has made you successful and why?

My values are important to me. I always treat my clients and others with respect and with integrity. It's important to me that if I say I am going to do something you know, I will follow through. One of my core values is to give back to my community. This allows me to do charitable work locally with The Sylvia Thomas Center in hopes that my community can be impacted by benefitting from how thankful I am for their support. I surround myself with clients that have very similar values and if a potential client does not fit my integrity or values I am comfortable letting them know I may not be the right coach for them.

How have you defined your voice in your market?

What sets me apart from my competition is my compassion for my clients. I learned from the coach/owner at the clinic that I trained with that treating clients like they are failures and not getting to know and thank them is not how I wanted to run my business. My clients will tell you that I never give up on them while I work to empower their lifelong success. Although they may have a slip while on the program, when they walk through my door and our coaching session begins, it is all about helping them to stay focused on their health goals. They know that I care about them and understand where they have been and where they are going so that they leave feeling empowered.

What would you advise someone who is struggling with building their brand?

I would highly suggest finding the right person or company that has experience as an expert in branding businesses. They need to understand your message and ensure it is consistent across all aspects of advertising, social media and web design. It is important that if a client is looking at any of these platforms they can say, "hey that is XYZ company" without even looking at the content.

Staying motivated when things don't seem to be coming together is a challenge at times. How do you motivate yourself? What would you advise someone else?

While being a business owner can have its struggles, I have learned that if I always look at the negative I will not move forward. I believe in offering those struggles up to God for His guidance. I make lists of what works and what doesn't work and I have a life business coach that helps. My coach teaches me how to work through challenges that pop up whether personally or professionally. I am also committed to scheduling time for the business homework my coach gives me so that I am working on my business not in my business.

What has been your most effective marketing tool / strategy and why?

When it comes to marketing, I have found that using my client's success stories works the best. I love the app RIPL as it allows me to show the success of my clients using video to show their success stories. I enjoy taking advantage of the local community papers to share our success's as well. The most effective ways I market currently are newsletters, special offer emails and getting my clients to refer their friends.

One of the biggest struggles women entrepreneurs have is how to price themselves. What advice would you share about pricing your services and offerings?

When I first started my business, I thought I needed to be priced lower than my competition. Over the years while working with my coach I have learned that my time is valuable. I bring and offer a lot more than many competitors for my clients. Once, I finally wrapped my head around that I increased my prices based on the value I truly bring. I have not lost a client because of the change in price. I have incorporated packages based on the amount of time a client will need our services and find that the clients love the options.

What advice would you give to a woman entrepreneur who is ready to take her business to the next level?

I still am looking for new ways to take my business to the next level. I am beginning to offer coaching via the internet or phone. I am currently looking at doing more with the guidance of my coach as I am currently setting up on site nationwide seminars, web seminars, and virtual coaching.

What "must have" resources would you recommend someone use in their business?

Looking back at when I started my business, I am glad that I chose something that I'm passionate about. That allows me to make an impact on my community and by doing this it brings me great joy especially because I am well known (sometimes too well) because of my commitment to help others in our program through scholarships.

What makes you a woman that is making an impact?

It's interesting that I am writing this book now. I am currently reflecting and prayerful about where and what my next step should be. My business has enabled me to help a charity that is dear to my heart called The Sylvia Thomas Center. We help families that are adopting from the foster care program. We help with pre-and post-adoption support. Over the years working with them, my heart has been pulled to do more with them in a larger capacity. I am not sure where that is going to bring me, but finding a way to do both is what I am asking God's guidance for. I would love to offer more on site seminars for our programs enabling me to be more of a mobile health coach. I know that there is a path set for me already and I will do my best to listen to what God places on my heart. As with all of us, our stories are always evolving and my chapter

Learn more about Pearl Chiarenza

My name is Pearl Chiarenza from Tampa, Florida. I am currently the owner of Bodyworks Health & Wellness Center in Brandon and Lakeland, Fl. I have been married to my wonderful husband Chuck for 30 years and we have two wonderful boys Matt (19) and Nate (17).

My journey to opening my weight loss clinic began when I lost 57lbs eight years ago. Providing one to one coaching on a healthier way of living, allows me to give back to my community, empower our dieters to make healthy changes and teach them the tools to maintaining their success.

Website: www.bodyworkshwc.com

ERIN WEBER
Certified Integrative Nutrition Health Coach

Tell us a little about yourself. We want to learn about the person behind the brand.

I grew up on the Northside of Chicago, Illinois in the most wonderful neighborhood. The years were filled with sweet memories, even though my dad left the picture while my younger sister and I were in elementary school. Our mom, grandparents and family friends made sure we thrived. I believe some of the most valuable lessons are learned through adversity. Perseverance is a strong attribute that was laid in my foundation through those times.

I attempted to maintain a 'real world' job as an Art Director at an advertising agency, after college; but the stress and politics was much more than I expected. I left corporate America sobbing, scared and with little direction of my next move. The message was made abundantly clear that everything was going to be alright, when I got into the car, after my last day, and "Better Life" by Keith Urban was playing on the radio. I began to laugh out loud knowing God wanted me to have faith in that uncertain moment. Go ahead; look up the lyrics. It's funny how sometimes it clicks and you're ready to hear a message, loud and clear. There was no mistaking that one.

My rock, Ben became the co-pilot I counted on. He gave me the encouragement I was missing, taught me to be proud of who I am, see what good I do have to offer and how I could choose to grow from failure with a new mindset. God's hand was every bit present in our meeting. After a 4 year, long-distance courtship, we married in 2005. We chose to relocate to Dallas, Texas just two months later where Ben had a solid, lucrative career with a mortgage industry leader. Our future was bright.

After a happy and healthy pregnancy in 2007, we welcomed our first son into the world. Everything revolved around him until a short-time later when we faced unexpected challenges. The housing market bubble burst and Ben was faced with abrupt unemployment. We pulled together in crisis mode, taking odd Craigslist jobs and clipping coupons. Adopting a no matter what attitude, ditching the excuses and finding solutions helped us shift our situation from dismal to hopeful. That baby boy was counting on us. Failure wasn't an option. That rocky time ultimately made us stronger, individually and as a couple.

In the years to come, we got back on our feet financially; but life was still far from perfect. A string of miscarriages left me void of health and faith. I struggled with the lack of answers and developed a *why me* perspective on life. I didn't know how to cope with this sort of failure. Many told me it wasn't my fault but what was I supposed to do with that inner guilt and grief? I prayed for clarity.

I found an online support group of women who also found themselves on the same, scary path I had come to discover. I wasn't alone in my anger or disappointment. My perspective began to expand when I learned others were dealing (or not dealing) with the emotional turmoil too. This was the beginning of my interest in helping others through their own health confusion and how I would come to lean on the Lord. I wondered... could my story help someone else avoid a similar path or support them through their own journey? What if this is what it's all about?

It would be many months later (which felt like eternity), that we would find our own bumpy, yet rewarding, road. They call the birth following a miscarriage a rainbow baby because of God's promise after the storm. In 2011, we received that most precious gift when our youngest son was born. Life was sweet once again.

Several months after my second son's birth, my health began to plummet into a valley. I was not a stranger to those feelings however, this time they lasted longer and impacted my quality of life. I sought the help of doctors, but was assured a thorough blood panel revealed nothing internally was terribly out of balance. So why was I stuck in a constant fog, dismal mood, my hair was falling out, weight increasing and energy lacking? I couldn't think clearly or sleep well. I ended up with more prescriptions but no clear answers or route to finding a solution. The journey ahead felt hopeless. I was breathing, but not living. Alas, I arrived at rock bottom early in 2014. My rock of a husband swept in to care for our young boys.

My persistent thought was that I didn't want my kids remembering me that way but I didn't know how to snap out of it either. The memory of how detached I became still brings a lump to my throat. I don't know where I was headed but it wasn't good. Facing a scary fork in the road; it was time to choose. I listened to the deep-down whisper that said "choose HOPE" and gave one last push of courage to truck down that muddy, uncharted path; for my kid's sake.

To make a conscious shift, I raised awareness in all my lifestyle choices. From dietary habits to physical fitness, people I interacted with, my career, financial stability and family. Crowding out the bad stuff with good; little by little, the small changes added up. I started to feel better. I was healing in a holistic way, and didn't even know it. I just listened to the messages my body was giving me.

The re-awakening of my passion for life was nothing short of spiritual. A ladder of hope was lowered to help me climb out of that deep hole. I couldn't contain the good news! I began telling anyone who would listen about the steps I had taken, activities I tried, products I used and the passion it awoke in me. Even if they didn't have as far to climb, maybe my friends could benefit from some of those tools too? Maybe they would even like my help? Exploring those thoughts led me back to school and the most rewarding career I've ever embarked on.

My family and I are in an amazing chapter of life. I stopped looking for "the catch" and started embracing it for all it's worth. I know my health, happiness and abundance are aligned for prosperity. We've got big plans and I can't wait to watch them unfold.

Share with us what your business is and why you wanted to start this business.

It was made clear to me at a young age that having an advanced degree must play a large role in my future. Until high school, I thought everyone *had* to go to college. I completed my BFA in Graphic Design at Northern Illinois University in 2001, yet I knew I was destined for something else that would fulfill my heart more.

After my health hit rock bottom in 2014, and I learned to rise again, my desire to help others achieve their own idea of health and happiness was heightened. I decided to develop my passion into a career and so I attended The Institute of Integrative Nutrition in 2015 to become a Certified Integrative Nutrition Health Coach. I dug deeper, learning how health all comes together, how to empower others with confidence to reach and maintain their own success, how positive choices, mindset and a holistic approach all rotate from the same wheel house. I was, and still am, in love with the journey that led me to this point. The career that it helped me unfold is just an added bonus.

Early on, I integrated a brand of supplements into my lifestyle that shifted my success in a way others hadn't. I felt the nudge to start sharing my story then. I had a toolset at my disposal that was a catalyst to recovering my own health. How could I keep something like that to myself? I had to share!

I realized my two arms could only stretch so wide so I began linking arms with a team who related. We shared the stories and asked others to consider joining us too. The messages spread and a seemingly accidental business was born.

Almost 2 1/2 years later, I now have an amazing team of change makers who are dedicated, caring and looking to make an impact on those they care most about too. I've developed a thriving business and learned to lead people to success in health and business. I'm often humbled to find myself ranked among the top performers however, it's the happiness and personal growth I've experienced that are my prized gifts. Having a product partner has not only added to the tools I can offer my clients in their own journey but I now see the big picture in how our impact will ripple out into the world.

What have you learned about yourself in running your business?

I CAN do hard things! I use to be a ball of excuses; an expert at figuring out how to get around obstacles instead of trucking through them. In the end, it didn't work and I had to go back and slop through the mud anyway. I now take that responsibility head on. I am the only one who can change that internal limiting belief and break down the barriers that I let stand in my way. It took a long time to learn, but once I did, I began looking for solutions instead of excuses.

What three things do you wish you would have known when you started?

First, let me say that I don't wish that my path was any different. The journey is where, and how, I was awakened to the possibilities of being a better me, for living life on my terms and for getting to where I am today. That said, here's some insight to what I would have liked to have known at an earlier stage.

1) Mindset trumps skill set; it is a practice. It takes time to refocus and retrain mental and emotional defaults we've believed our whole lives. Practicing a good habit consistently, like repeating positive affirmations, can help crowd the bad messages out. Personal development is a non-negotiable activity in my every day routine. Whether reading, practicing affirmations or meditation, I value the reflection time for growth; it's like a mental workout strengthening my brain.

2) No one's journey is the same. Give gratitude and attention to what you DO have vs. what you think you should; what is working vs. what is not; what success you have achieved vs. what you think you should have. Stop "shoulding" on yourself! You ARE already enough. You'll see more of what you focus on, so find the good. There is ALWAYS something good. Try journaling 3 things you're grateful for each day if this seems like a tough task.

3) Progress, not perfection. It's the little ideas and actions that lead up to bigger ones. Celebrate those. If you want to win, learn from your failures and make changes. The only way to lose is to quit. No winner is without failure.

What 3 characteristics describe what has made you successful and why?

Everyone has a different idea of success so this one is difficult to box up. For some it's a money thing or title or lines on their resume. I have a completely different take. I like to look at success as mindset meets action. When I have a goal, yes, there's a reachable target or success point however, I find the true success comes in the journey to reaching it. The mindset, actions, time and energy you put forth are all small steps that add up to reaching that success. You're rarely able to hit the jackpot in one chance. Putting daily practice into habits on how to persevere through the ups and downs, having a support network of positive influencers to lean on and learning from mistakes, helps me to keep finding my idea of success.

How have you defined your voice in your market?

When I took responsibility in healing my own body, mind and spirit, I regained confidence in myself. A big part of my voice comes from the lessons learned on that journey. I find strength in sharing my story and want to help others discover their voice too. I've walked the walk and remember the trials and hurdles all too well. I relate to a lot of moms out there who are just doing their best. Juggling life, stress and health is no easy fete. Exposing the humor in our common imperfection is empowering. So, what if the dishes stack up, the clothes aren't put away and dinner is burnt? The struggle is real, sister...and I don't mind being the one to point it out. My truth is progress, not perfection. We need more grace to live a messy, but happy, life.

What would you advise someone who is struggling with building their brand?

I believe your brand is about owning your truths. Being vulnerable in exploring your real story is what will make it take shape. Ask yourself the hard questions and set some goals. What do you see yourself accomplishing? Where? When? Why? Who are the people you'll want by your side or helping you? I believe it's in casting the vision that you'll begin to see the steps you'll need to take to shape your brand.

Staying motivated when things don't seem to be coming together is a challenge at times. How do you motivate yourself? What would you advise someone else?

Motivation is something that should stem from *your why*. Why do you do what you do? Why you want to change things, overcome obstacles and reach your goals. *Your why is your driver.*

My why is an idea that makes me pop out of bed in the morning and do one more thing before calling it a night. It's deeply rooted, makes me cry and keeps me motivated. I cast a vision of what it will take to reach that big, audacious goal. The people involved, the money it will take and what life will feel like when it all comes together. All the details. I wrote it down and then recorded the story in a voice memo that I can playback from anywhere. I also tune into motivational videos I've compiled in playlist on YouTube. Motivation is fully connected to your mindset.

Paint a clear picture first then write it down, record it, make a dream board, or find a person who can help inspire you back into action. We're all motivated in different ways. I say find what works for you and build a portfolio of outlets that you can turn to when you feel like you want to give up.

What has been your most effective marketing tool / strategy and why?

Word-of-mouth advertising has been my sole strategy in growing my business. I didn't purposely set out to grow from my health crisis in a way that developed a business so organically, as I began to tell friends what happened and how, a business opportunity appeared and I ran with it. I appreciate the grass roots campaign that's gotten me this far and helped me achieve this much. My network of friends stems from all parts of the globe, so social media is, and has been, my most effective marketing tool. I'm able to connect to my friends (and their friends), build upon my network through referrals and warm introductions and utilize many streams of communication. Sharing pictures, stories and videos has allowed me to be open in how I share parts of my story. I've found the more real and authentic I am, the more my audience connects with my message and is inspired to take action.

One of the biggest struggles women entrepreneurs have is how to price themselves. What advice would you share about pricing your services and offerings?

I think women struggle with this because we're natural caregivers. When you love what, you do, it's easy to want to share that love, anytime, anywhere. We often feel a sincere "thank you" is plenty of pay. I'm singing to the choir here as I still find myself struggle with this one. I used to feel the financial investment someone would make in me was more pressure to deliver big results. What I found couldn't be further from the truth. People wanted to invest in me for the value I brought to their life, not just for their waist size at the conclusion of a health program. People remember more about how you make them feel than the products you deliver.

My advice for women struggling with pricing confusion is twofold. One, realize your efforts, energy and time ARE valuable. You do deserve the financial reward of the investment you make in someone too. Two, connect with industry friends and ask for help. What does their price list look like? How did they come to find that magic number? Trial and error may reveal what your target market is willing to spend however, I'd bet there's friends out there who can help you narrow it down.

What advice would you give to a woman entrepreneur who is ready to take her business to the next level?

Invest more in your imports (mindset, balance, joy, relationships) than your exports (products, programs, services). Personal development is the best time investment you can make to keep yourself balanced inside. Internal imbalances can manifest through your mood, physical appearance, sleep disruptions, eating behaviors and so on. You can't pour from an empty cup. Those stressors will affect your business and relationships. Focus inward when looking to transition to the next level or get off a plateau. Whether it's your health or business we're talking about, the investment is the same.

What "must have" resources would you recommend someone use in their business?

I think the most important resource someone can utilize in business is finding the right support network. Surround yourself with a community of caring friends, family, industry mentors and those who encourage you. The ones who bring out your best qualities, inspire creativity and action. The ones who are open to hearing your business ideas, want to support you on your journey, cheer for you, help you find solutions, hold you accountable, foster a positive outlook and encourage you to grow from failure. My support network is my most valuable asset in my business and life. I would not have been able to grow if it weren't for their unconditional support and nudging through the mud. My network inspires me to be the best version of myself.

What makes you a woman that is making an impact?

It's funny the question is phrased this way because it feels a bit full circle. I named my team, Team IMPACT (I'M Passionate About Changing Today) after I came to a place in my business where I had to grow into a leader. It was a great time to evaluate how I taught my team to approach business, from a caretaker's position. Our foundation became to help inspire others to make positive choices for their health and happiness. My hope in growing a team is to link arms to share that message. Together, our ripple effect will be much greater than my two arms can reach. I feel honored to watch a lasting legacy of healthy lifestyles develop for my friend's families too.

Being a leader (as in a woman making an impact), doesn't mean being bossy, managerial or demanding control. I feel it's an internal responsibility to choose your own path, take the reins, change your behaviors and find your place in this world.

I'm a woman making an impact because I choose to change today. I make choices in every decision, to shift my life towards what makes me happiest. It's not a selfish act but rather a raised awareness that my behavior, intentional or not, has a ripple effect in the world. My health, mood and money are all currency to those choices. Hitting rock bottom helped me see the power of what negativity can do to a family. It was my wakeup call. A candle loses nothing by lighting another candle. I choose light and will share with anyone open to receiving it.

Wild card question! Share whatever you would like the women reading your story to know about you, your business, or your journey.

I shed my past when I chose that new path of hope, health and happiness. I see this chance as a gift, and renewed opportunity, to live life to the fullest...and share that message. My desire to help others is greater than my limiting fears of what others will say or think. It's a privilege to get to be the vessel that introduces someone to their own life-changing journey. I feel blessed and honored to get to do work I love, on my own terms. This chapter of life is one I never imagined.

If there's anything I've learned through my journey, it's that YOU have the chance to choose differently, at every moment. Whether it's your words, thoughts or actions, make conscience choices, listen to that little voice inside, be aware of the ripple effect you're sending out into your home, and the world. You ARE making an impact.

Learn more about Erin Weber

Erin Weber is a Certified Integrative Nutrition Health Coach who also has a BFA from Northern Illinois University. She is committed to empowering women to achieve their most vibrant lifestyle through a natural approach to wellness, emotional balance and other facets in the circle of life. Erin is frequently featured as a speaker and educator on nutrition & preventive wellness concepts. As a wife and busy mom of two boys; when she's not juggling everyday life, you can find her at the gym, enjoying the outdoors or traveling the world. She believes in a philosophy of "progress, not perfection."

Website: www.HealthEnergyHappiness.com

About the Compiler: Kimberly Pitts
Founder of UImpact & UImpact Publishing Group

Kimberly Pitts is both a Branding & Marketing Strategist and Developer. She is a change agent who is dedicated to helping entrepreneurs and small business owners through our strategic consulting services, creative expertise, and experiential events, we help our clients create game-changing brands to increase revenue, build authority status, and maximize impact. UImpact is tomorrow's branding company, today.

Anything but conventional, Kimberly's creative and innovative techniques will challenge you, encourage you, inspire and equip you to get to the place you desire, and deserve to be. Whether you are in the start-up stages of your business or you are ready to grow to the next level of success and expand your reach, Kimberly is here to provide expert mentoring to better position you and your business for greater influence.

UImpact / www.uimpact.net
UImpact Publishing Group / www.uimpactpublishing.com

Remember:

Your brand is much more interesting when it has heart and life behind it.

The story of your brand matters.

Made in the USA
Lexington, KY
09 February 2017